Unraveled

From Sibling Abuse to Sacred Self

a memoir

By Sherri A. Lynn

Unraveled
From Sibling Abuse to Sacred Self
A Memoir
Copyright © 2023 by Sherri A. Lynn

ISBN: 979-8-9865884-1-4

This work depicts actual events in the life of the author as truthfully as recollection permits and/or can be verified by research. Occasionally, dialogue consistent with the character or nature of the person speaking has been supplemented. All persons within are actual individuals; there are no composite characters. The names of some individuals have been changed to respect their privacy.

Content contained or made available through this book is not intended to and does not constitute legal or therapeutic advice and no attorney/therapist-client relationship is formed. The publisher and the author are providing this book and its contents on an "as is" basis. Your use of the information in this book is at your own risk.

Published by
Sherri A. Lynn
New Jersey

Cover design: Eric Labacz, labaczdesign.com

A Note to Readers:

This book contains themes surrounding generational abuse and addiction. Please practice self-care when reading this book and know that recovery is possible.

For the Silently Suffering Siblings still out there.
May you find your way
to peace, healing, and wholeness.
And to Marie,
for your courage and compassion
in introducing me to Sibling Abuse
and encouraging me on the path to recovery.

About the Cover

Choosing a cover for this book was almost as tough as writing the dedication for my first book. There were two submissions, equally powerful and worthy. The first symbolizes a young girl teetering in the middle of a frayed rope. It represents what my journey looks like having left dysfunction but not quite reaching safety yet.

The selected cover shows how I've allowed myself to be seen by the world, smiling in the face of defeat (as the newspaper photo from 1978 titled it). Emerging from the right side of that photo is the adult silhouette from my first book,

Smiling in the face of defeat

All My Heroes Have Fur, Fins & Feathers. What the newspaper photo and caption don't capture are the horrific events I'd suffered up until that point in my life. It doesn't show how playing team sports saved my life and kept me going. Softball made me feel part of something and provided a welcome break from the crazy I thought was normal. When I see that photo today, I am inspired. I realize that young woman is a courageous one, worthy of giving and receiving love. I also have so much respect and compassion for what she's *Unraveled* in this lifetime.

Thank you, Eric Labacz, for the design and Rich Pipeling for taking the original photo.

Contents

Chapter 36

Prologue

Childhood should be about questions and answers. Questions we ask our parents, our teachers, our siblings. Why am I here? Who am I supposed to be? Why do I feel like this? What does this mean? Can you explain this to me? Can you help me? Will I be OK? Why are you doing that? When a child stops asking questions, growing and learning are affected, and so is their sense of self.

Chaotic and consistently inappropriate childhood conditioning forced me to stop asking questions at a very young age. Being beaten by an angry, disconnected mother, ignored by an alcoholic father or incessantly and mercilessly ridiculed and tortured by an abusive sibling for being curious set the stage for a lifetime of figuring things out on my own—*usually the hard way!*

~~~

I truly didn't know what I didn't know and was too terrified to ask. Staying small and under the proverbial radar ensured my early life survival. It didn't take long to discover that when I kept other people happy, my life was easier. That way of "being" in the world worked well in many environments but it was exhausting, self-defeating, and soul-depleting. Internally, I started asking questions again in my early twenties.

What am I doing wrong? How did I get here? Why did this happen again? What am I missing? Where do I want to be? What do I need to learn? Why?

I started to occasionally hear soft whispers of navigational guidance inside my head. *Turn here, go this way, don't go that way, slow down, hurry.* The voice got louder, more frequent, and offered all kinds of things to take notice of. Life as I knew it was changing. The hypersensitivity I used as a child to stay safe had morphed into a special spiritual language. Guidance and information came by way of songs, scents, coins, paper money, animals, landscape, and so much more. I was developing a connection with spirit and my higher self that would lead me on a path to healing from and understanding my traumatic past.

While I still don't like much of what I suffered through, I have finally realized that I AM the person I always wished would show up for me. If you happen to see yourself on any of the following pages, my sincere hope is that you, too, find the path to healing and wholeness you've only ever dreamed of.

You are worthy and deserving.

Chapter 1
The First Time

Despite easily verifiable claims by my older sibling to the contrary, it was August 30, 1985. It was the tenth birthday of my mother's first grandchild, not the day after, as was told to the children. Those children, now well into their forties, still blindly believe their parent's lie (s). I understand how fear keeps them frozen; I was frozen with fear once, too.

I lay across the short side of the bottom bunk; my legs and the top of my body hung off opposite sides. One of Mom's hand crocheted afghans in a gold, orange, and brown chevron pattern was tossed in a bundle on the floor. I was distraught. I needed a sign—a sign that there was something more after death. And then it happened.

I was twenty years of age and had found my mother dead, supposedly of a massive heart attack. There was never an autopsy so one can't be a hundred percent sure. A lifetime of personal abuse prepared me to be cool, calm, and collected as I called the police who, in turn, dispatched the rescue squad. I could hear the emergency siren wail in the background while I was still on the phone.

When I walked in, the smell of the room and the color of her face were obvious signs she was gone. Before others arrived, I also noticed that the energy of the room itself was different. It was absent of life—her life.

My mind was sharp and laser-focused. I remembered my friend and her mom were off from work that day and that my twenty-seven-year-old sibling was taking some kind of required class to continue receiving free money from the government. Our dad was working. Calmly, I made the necessary calls and waited for everyone to appear.

Once on the scene the police and rescue personnel confirmed what I already knew to be true—my mom had been dead for hours. After the official pronouncement her body was taken to the funeral home. While waiting for the rest to arrive, I continued making calls, including to my dad's work. The postmaster had to send someone to locate my dad on his mail route. I remember he arrived thinking the "big emergency" was that one of my cats had gotten hit by a car.

The next person to tell was our grandmother. We agreed it was best to go rather than call her at work so one of us could drive her car home. And we did. Later somebody decided that I was in shock and needed tranquilizers. Being raised to believe that everybody else was smarter and knew what was best for me, I took what they gave me and as often as they did.

I was bounced around from place to place like a bad penny that day. I remember sitting on the couch at one of my grandmother's adult foster kid's homes while they talked like I wasn't in the room. They spoke as if they were the ones who found her, like their lives were the ones whose life had just been turned upside down. At some point, when that group had enough of me, I was returned to the house I grew up in.

The next steps of planning my mother's funeral were taking place: clothing, insurance, flowers, obituary, pictures, funeral home appointment, and the next level of phone calls. The story of what happened was repeated over and over, sometimes more than once to the same person. I retreated to the back bedroom and stretched myself across the bottom bunk, dangling off both ends.

I stared at Mom's crumpled afghan on the floor. It was a beginner's stitch in a simple pattern. The colors were very popular in the 1970s. Interestingly enough, Mom's 1970 Pontiac Lemans was gold. While looking at the afghan, I noticed its placement on the tongue and groove wooden floor. I paid particular attention to how far away it was from the next board, then whispered. "Are you here?"

The energy of the room changed in a way I never had experienced. "Are you here?" I asked again, a little louder. A weird tingling feeling washed over me. It felt like the answer was "yes" but I needed more proof. What would THAT feel like? To communicate with the other side? I steadied myself and demanded. "Mom, if that's you, move the afghan—move the afghan over the line."

"HOLY SHIT!!! She's here! Mommy's here!" I yelled so loudly everyone came running up the hall to check on me. With complete joy and certainty I pointed to the afghan and told what had just happened. From the looks of disbelief I received you would have thought I had just described some fantastic scene out of a horror flick where the afghan was picked up whirled around by some unknown entity and set back down on the other side of the room. It wasn't like that. It was incredibly slow and deliberate. From start to finish the afghan moved maybe an inch. How far didn't really matter to me. The fact was I asked my dead mother to move it, and move it she did!

My "family" began taking care of me by feeding me tranquilizers like M&M's. They thought I had lost my mind. Had I? Or was I coming into my own? Time would certainly tell, and it would be years before the pieces of my gift would unravel and start falling into place.

Chapter 2

Finding My Way Part 1

I….

Felt…

Awful…

My mother's death, and life as I knew it, sent me into further turmoil. Others continued to make decisions for me—and I let them. I let them because I didn't know differently. "They" decided I could no longer live in the house where I found my mother dead. "They" decided I would "go crazy" if I stayed. And how would I manage anyway? My sibling was already wringing their hands at the thought of collecting "rent" from me. It was a way for them to avoid joining the workforce to make their own money. Since they now owned half a house, they were no longer eligible for free money every month. Live free with dad, collect rent from me, and stay home and watch TV all day. Yeah, no, that wasn't happening.

The house was purchased with assistance from my grandmother; since she was the life insurance beneficiary, she didn't want it sold. Since I "wasn't allowed" to live there anymore, my sibling continued wringing their hands at the new and improved prospect of being a landlord—while I would be expected to take care of everything. Honestly, it was a tiny little house with rooms set in a row that would have probably just brought in enough rent to cover expenses. For the next several months, I would go there a few times a day to care for my two dogs and three cats. I didn't go crazy, but I did feel things when I was there. I felt lots of things.

I felt guilt and shame and fear and sadness. There were days when I felt angry, too. I was angry that there was no room at Dad's or Grandmom's, and I was stuck sharing a bedroom with a friend in her mother's house, and that my things were in a house on the other side of town. I was angry that everybody "cared" so much about me before Mom's body was in the ground, and then it felt as if they left me high and dry. Sure, I was grateful I *had* a place to stay but it was not permanent, and it certainly wasn't ideal. I kept beer in the fridge at Mom's house and began abusing it to cope with my situation. At some point I heard the little voice in my head say, "You're on your own, you have to figure this out."

Panic washed over me when I smelled heating oil during one morning house check. At some point during the night the heating unit had failed, leaving behind puddles of fuel oil. It stunk, and my heart raced at the thought of it catching fire while I was there. Back then I had no idea how house things worked or where the emergency shutoffs were. I called the repair guy, my useless sibling, my grandmom, and my work to let them know I wasn't coming in. *You're on your own, you can't keep doing this, this house has to go.*

Three cats and one dog were relocated to my dad's and the smaller dog, a poodle, was relocated to my grandmother's, despite her protests. It seemed like forever but in just under a year Mom's house was sold. My grandmother never forgave me. I suspect my sibling was disappointed, too, since now they had to get a real job. Armed with a high school education, some part- time office cleaning experience, and an ability to manipulate others, my sibling arrived at our dead mother's work, had the audacity to ask for our mother's job, and got it—probably sat at her same desk, too!

Meanwhile, I moved out of my friend's house, into Dad's UNFINISHED basement, took on a second job, joined the rescue squad, and started saving money. I worked from 8:30 a.m. to 11:00 p.m. five nights a week—and drank like a fish on weekends. Eventually, I needed knee surgery and had to give up the second job.

Despite "only" having a high school education, my ridiculously strong work ethic allowed for two department changes and eventually landed me in the computer department with lots of potential for growth. At twenty-six years of age, I started making enough money to open a retirement account and bought a house. It was a fixer-upper, not in the best neighborhood, but it was mine! "You're on your own, look at you!"

I was elected to leadership roles at the rescue squad and continued to get promoted at work. Being almost in constant motion kept the voices muffled. It also gave the outward appearance that I was OK and doing well. My drinking evolved into regular blackouts and continued for a few years. Internally, I struggled and used busyness and alcohol to keep it tamed. That was how I coped.

At twenty-nine a series of events landed me in the rooms of Alcoholics Anonymous®. A breast cancer diagnosis two years later blessed me with a wake-up call. It was the first time in my life that I consciously put myself, my health, and my happiness above absolutely everything and everyone else. "This feels really good."

A few years later Hurricane Floyd ripped through our town. The basement in Mom's old house filled with muddy flood waters that eventually seeped through to the first floor. *Aren't you glad you sold that house? You'd be cleaning up that mess by yourself. Maybe Grandmom will finally forgive you.* Fat chance. I still think she felt somehow *I* was responsible for my mother's heart attack; somehow it was ***my*** fault she was overweight, drank, ate fatty foods, made bad choices, and smoked like a chimney. Just take it in, don't say a thing. "***You*** know the truth, you know ***your*** truth."

Chapter 3
Finding My Way Part 2

Looking back, it wasn't *all* bad. I learned things and had a lot of fun along the way, even when those things came at the expense of myself or others. I have vivid childhood memories of playing cards and board games with cousins. It was always my sibling and me against the cousins, and always at the kitchen table, never on the floor. *Always* at the kitchen table! We played at the table so my sibling and I could pass playing cards or Monopoly money or property deeds to each other under the table with our feet. My sibling had to win however possible, even cheating. Truth be told, my sibling would cheat themselves playing solitaire. I'm ashamed to admit that it felt good having my sibling treat me nicely during those brief encounters. The irony here is that my sibling's adult children believed *me* to be the cheater. Funny, considering I'm seven years younger.

As adults, my sibling and I also ganged up on and mocked others, including people we dated. We would do things to set them up to look stupid while camping or hiking. Being new to these activities, the friends believed just about every word we said and would act accordingly. I remember once witnessing a demonstration on how to clean stuck food out of a frying pan with a piece of a tree. My partner at the time thought they were watching some real-life camping hack until my sibling passed the pan and branch over while trying to contain their laughter. These events may have seemed funny at the surface, but the fact is they were mean-spirited through and through. I didn't know it then, but I *definitely* know it now. In my heart I have asked for forgiveness for behaving the way I did. In the process I have learned to stick up for the underdog, and sometimes that underdog is *me!*

~~~

The "not all bad" sentiment holds true for my drinking, too. I met my first live-in girlfriend at a bar. She called me out for liking women, and I fiercely denied it—until the second time I saw her and was half in the bag. We couldn't get enough of each other; eventually, she left somebody else and moved in with me. Our lives back then consisted of mostly drinking, bad decisions, and chaos, but we were happy. In fact, I thought we had a good relationship because we didn't fight. Honestly, I just gave in the way my dad taught me about conflict resolution with my sibling. I let my partner have her way most of the time to keep the peace. Fortunately, we both started to realize how out of control our drinking had gotten. Fate intervened. She received a DUI that landed us both in Alcoholics Anonymous®, but that doesn't mean we took it seriously right away.

We still weren't convinced that we were "powerless over alcohol" or that our lives "had become unmanageable." For a while we attended meetings during the week and tried recruiting others from the bar on the weekends. After all, all our "good friends" were drunks, too! Eventually, we managed to string together ninety days and then more. Before we knew it we were also running one of the local meetings. Life was good for about two years before I received a breast cancer diagnosis.

It's funny how that happened. I know with every ounce of my being that if I had still been drinking, my story would have ended there. Instead, I took the diagnosis as a sign, a clear sign, to do the things I wanted to do and see and experience before I died.

My partner and I and anyone who wanted to join us started actively working through a bucket list. For years we traveled and cruised and participated in adventures like winter camping, dog sledding, sky diving, ballooning, white water rafting, and so much more. When we weren't working we were on the go doing fun things. She also insisted we spend more time with my sibling.

"That's how close families do things," she said.

Eventually, it got to the point where my sibling was almost constantly with us. My pleas for activities without my sibling were ignored.

There were other times when it felt like my partner didn't hear me or take me seriously. When we vacationed with *her* family I would often ask for just one day without them—just one day for us to do as we pleased. They were nice enough people, but I didn't want to spend every single minute of my vacation with them. Taking five hours to decide on a restaurant for dinner isn't exactly my idea of a good time. I asked but didn't know how to hold firm or get my needs met. I only knew something didn't feel right. Frustrated, I would internally beat myself up for not handling it better. What's wrong with me? Was I asking for too much?

A voice inside my head whispered, "You're not going to be with her forever. Just wait and see."

A series of events suspended our adventures and put major strains on our relationship. Her stepfather had a stroke, and she flew to Florida for several weeks to care for him. When she returned her half-brother moved in with us for a while. Her real dad in Pennsylvania was hospitalized and ended up dying, and then her mother received a cancer diagnosis in Florida. Since she refused surgery and treatment of any kind, her fate was pretty much sealed, and she died in March 2002. I made another trip out to Florida to join my partner and her family for the funeral service.

In June 2002, only three months later, my dad was rushed

to the hospital at midnight. He had had a "simple" hernia surgery earlier that day but wasn't feeling well.

My sibling called to tell me his symptoms, and I said, "Call the rescue squad; I'll be right there."

My so-called partner mumbled "OK," rolled over, and fell back to sleep when I attempted to explain what was going on.

I arrived to find my dad clutching his chest, gasping for breath, wearing striped button-down pajamas soaked with sweat. No doubt he was having a heart attack less than twelve hours post-surgery. My sibling was standing nearby stupefied. It's hard to know whether the look was due to muscle relaxers taken earlier or if it was their usual look of helplessness.

The police arrived first, then the rescue squad, and then advanced life support.

Dad knew. While he was lying in the bed he pointed to his cheek and told me to give him a kiss, "just in case."

Calmly, I said, "For what? You're not going anywhere; let's get this oxygen on you. It will help you breathe."

I had always wondered, if I had been trained at the time, would I have been able to save my mom? And there I was, with my dad, actively watching him have a heart attack. The greatest chance for survival lies in the "golden hour." His care began within minutes, and I helped. We were soon on our way to the hospital. My sibling rode in the ambulance, and I followed behind in my car.

In the emergency room the cardiologist with the bedside manner of a rock told my sibling and me, "Well, we can try to put in an external pacemaker but it's not going to work. He's gonna die either way."

We decided that it was better to try something rather than nothing and agreed to the pacemaker. The procedure was done in the ER and only took a few minutes.

"All done. You can go in and see him now."

As soon as I walked in the room, I noticed a familiar feeling, the feeling that I was in a room absent of life. This time it was absent of *Dad's* life. I looked at the doctor and told him what I already knew to be true. "He's dead."

They called a code but I knew it wouldn't do anything. It didn't.

I can't remember how or when I told the person I shared a bed with that my dad died. Trauma can do that to you. I do know that the next morning she got up and went to work like it was any other day. Some would argue that I didn't "ask" her to come with me; others would say that we "teach people how to treat us." Still others would just say, "it's horrible she wasn't there with you." I made the excuse that she probably couldn't handle it because her mom had just died. Meanwhile, my little voice used her outdoor volume when she asked, "WHAT....THE....F*#K? Who does that?"

"The same person that doesn't attend the first viewing and shows up late to the second," was the answer.

Not long after Dad's funeral my "partner" was spending more and more time weekends *at her aunt's house in Brooklyn.* Something didn't feel right. I'd asked if everything was OK but received mumbles in return. One day I asked her to help put a lawn mower in my trunk to take to my dad's house because my left-handed sibling wore out the cord on Dad's mower and the grass needed to be cut. I got a whiff of a familiar scent—alcohol. When questioned, my partner looked away and denied it. I pressed. Finally, she admitted to drinking Mike's Hard Lemonade.

"That's ALCOHOL!" I shouted back.

I was nine years sober at that time and had just lost my dad suddenly. The voice inside my head said, "Nobody is going to threaten your sobriety—nobody." The words spilled out of my mouth: "I want you OUT. NOW!"

It was the first time in my life I voiced a hard boundary with someone and held to it!

It.

Felt.

Awful!

Chapter 4

Finding My Way Part 3

Here you are again, feeling awful. What is going on?
You've been unhappy with her and the relationship for a long time.
It's been exhausting. You keep showing up for her, and she's
stopped showing up for you. She's clearly miserable and stopped
showing up for herself—and thinks drinking is going to fix it.

You know *this.* You *know* this relationship has run its
course. You know *she's dragging you down and holding you back.*
Then why are you feeling bad for finally *setting a hard boundary*
and kicking her out? Why?

~~~

Loss, Grief, Sadness, Loneliness, and Abandonment. They
can make you or break you. They are some of the best ingredients
in my own personal recipe for change and growth. Honestly, I
don't ever remember making changes when things were "good" or
"comfortable." Change for me has always come when I've been
frustrated. Frustrated with me, frustrated with someone else, or
frustrated with the way something was being done. I'd then find
myself being frustrated for being frustrated. And that's frustrating!

When I was in my late thirties I honestly didn't know what
I didn't know. By society's "rules," I was doing great—even
though inside I didn't feel so great. Society wants you to be
gainfully employed, own a home, be self-sufficient, give back to
your community, be active. I was or had all those things and more.

So why wasn't I happy? What was missing? Did I need a "person" to make me feel happy and complete?

Friends. I just need to keep myself busy with friends and keep myself distracted. I spent so much of my time with a friend my ex accused me of cheating. "OMG!" I would say. "I'm not the one that cheated on my partner. That was you. She's *just* my friend!"

I am ashamed to admit I was completely clueless that this "friend" really *did* want more than friendship from me. I was oblivious until the evening a good night hug went on longer than normal. The following night the long hug was followed by a deep sigh. *Uh oh*, I thought to myself. *What do I do with this? How does this feel?*

I reasoned that "friends first" *might* be the secret ingredient to a healthy relationship, unlike the last one that started in a drunken stupor and lasted nearly ten years. The attention I started to receive felt good and healthy. The newness and secrecy also felt fun; she was far in the closet, and I was hesitant to broadcast anything too soon for fear of jinxing it. Having been repeatedly taught as a youngster that everyone else knew what was best for me, I rolled with it.

Suffice it to say, in time a really good friendship was destroyed. That situation resulted in the fracturing and eventual loss of several other friendships I believed were solid. Trust and loyalty as I knew them were simply words. It ended badly *but* I became much clearer about what I *didn't* want!

The "next one" was much better! Kind, gentle, selfless, and caring—she was the one who insisted I "call someone" and get myself into therapy. My life felt like such a mess but I didn't know why—outwardly, everything was amazing but inside, I hurt. I remember sitting in my kitchen in tears, terrified to make the call. Nonconfrontational by nature, my "next one" put her foot down and said we weren't going anywhere that day until I did! Romantically, that one didn't work out either, but we will *always* be special friends and *always* be there for one another. We ended it amicably like loving adults.

~~~

I was afraid to make the call because my first exposure to therapy years earlier was a disaster. The idea I should go came from a former friend who suggested I use *her* therapist. So I did. And so did my longtime partner. This "therapist" worked out of her home and only took cash, no insurance. That's a definite red flag to me now! Not having a clue how therapy worked then, I followed the counselor's lead. The first visit wasn't so bad, but the second visit was a little weird. She seemed more excited to show off her new kitchen cabinets than address my needs. Further, she was put off when I suggested we start my session instead of admiring the cabinetry. My third visit was derailed by really bad weather and her obvious anger when I called to cancel because of it. In time I came to believe this lady was more of a wacko than a therapist. I vowed "never again."

Many years later my first "real" therapist gently took the edge of the ball of yarn that represented my life and started unraveling. "Aubrey" had her work cut out and got me to look at things differently. She constantly challenged many of my beliefs and regularly gave me homework. I had no idea how hard some of it was going to be. The one thing that kept me coming back were her dogs: two beautiful golden retrievers that seemed to know exactly what I needed. Many times I was happier to see them than my therapist!

In addition to unraveling, I started to put pieces of myself back together: to make changes, find my voice, and get intentional about what I wanted and where I was headed. I saw *Aubrey (and her dogs)* on and off for a few years. We unraveled as much as I was ready for. I gained insight about my choices and behavior. I also started to gather effective tools for coping, dealing with, and healing from the ugly that surfaced up until that point in my life. I started to listen to myself and pay closer attention to how I felt and what I needed and wanted.

Chapter 5

There's a Manual?

I'm a "doer." Always have been. I just jump in and figure it out or make it up as I go along. That's exactly how I "do" life. One of the earliest memories involves my first bike. It was a navy blue girl's bike from Sears with a white banana seat and chrome sissy bar. I don't know how old I was. I'm willing to bet barely age five. I'd tired of the training wheels limiting tight turns and wanted them off.

As a youngster, I was often alone—Dad was out delivering mail, Mom was cleaning or cooking, and sibling was god-knows-where. Since an improperly timed request for anything could result in being screamed at or beaten, I had learned very early in life *not* to ask anybody for anything. The instilled belief was that only weak and helpless people couldn't do things for themselves, which was a bad thing.

Thankfully, doing things with my hands seemed to come naturally. Even using hand tools came easily. I located wrenches in the garage, tipped my bike onto its side on the walk in front of our house, and got to work. I don't remember it being hard or taking long at all before my training wheels were off. Some days that story empowers me, and other days it makes me very sad. Learning NOT to depend on others was hard-wired into me early but, even worse, where was everybody for this milestone achievement? Who was going to hold the back of my seat? Take pictures? Celebrate this big deal? Who cared enough about me to witness and document this big event? Some days I still apologize to my younger self for that day, and I remind her that there are interested, engaging, and caring people out there, somewhere.

Most of my life has been done that same way—without a manual. I have jumped into all kinds of opportunities, situations, obligations, projects, commitments, appointments, and relationships without so much as a second thought. Honestly, I am ashamed to admit this but for much of my life I never even *knew* I had choices. Being yelled at for the stupidest of infractions, beaten for no reason, punished, and being forced to go places I didn't want to and then expected to hug ill-intentioned, alcohol, and smoky smelling adults all branded me with the belief that what I wanted or needed didn't matter. "You get what you get and you like it." I was also taught that saying "no" or setting boundaries was simply not an option. The really creepy part in all this is that no one in my family was affectionate. No one. So why was I being forced to hug and kiss people I didn't want to? A direct result of this contradictory conditioning was that I was incredibly uncomfortable with the social norm for greeting people warmly way into adulthood. After yet another failed relationship, it was time to start reading the manuals.

By this time I had come to understand that I had some deep-seated issues and beliefs because of my traumatic, abusive, and neglectful childhood. I started reading and working on them several years ago. What I hadn't yet unraveled was how all that crazy would affect every single part of my life, especially relationships. Being touch, attention, and affection starved, coupled with the belief that I was supposed to "get what I get and like it," set me up for more of the same insanity.

Chapter 6

Patterns, Patience, and Picture Painting

Sometimes signs "stand alone," and sometimes they are part of a bigger picture. Over time I have learned that it is incredibly important to pay attention to patterns and have patience when spirit is helping to paint a bigger picture.

My Aunt Mary rewarded those closest to her with a fifty-cent piece whenever our name made the local newspaper (for something good). She kept a giant stash to mark occasions like making the honor roll, graduating, doing something good in sports or for the community, or getting elected. You get the picture. Having been involved in many things, I had personally accumulated quite a few of them before she died back in 2005.

I follow and support a number of rescues and animal charities—too many to mention. I've noticed that once you are on one list, the requests for donations multiply like rabbits. Imagine my surprise when I received a new request from a Tiger Rescue with a fifty-cent piece showing through the window of the envelope! My heart and thoughts went immediately to my Aunt Mary. As someone who regularly gets messages from people on the other side, I just chalked it up to a "hello, I'm thinking about you." Little did I know what that fifty-cent piece was actually lining up for another family member.

Coming from an incredibly homophobic family isn't easy. To my knowledge only two of us are "out." I suspect there are others but, for whatever reason, they remain in the proverbial closet. Anyhow, fast-forward a few months after the fifty-cent piece arrived in my mail. I was asked to co-officiate my second cousin's wedding in Michigan. To say I was elated would be the understatement of the year. I accepted and got to work on the ceremony with the other officiant.

My co-officiant already had a draft ceremony written so we had an awesome starting point. One of the things I included in the draft was an acknowledgment and remembrance section. In it we acknowledged the people who had died that were of particular importance to both grooms. Naturally, we acknowledged my cousin's grandmother, to whom he fondly referred to as "Nana." If you've been following along, you already know that "Nana" was also my Aunt Mary.

~~~

I find coins all the time. I mean truly—ALL THE TIME. Daily and multiple times a day, in fact. I have a relationship with coins and their messages that most people probably wouldn't understand. It is a skill that has taken time and practice to develop. When I find a coin, the very first thing I do is express gratitude. The more I do this, the more I feel a divine love inside me that radiates outside my physical body. It literally lights me up from the inside out. The feeling is fantastic. I've been taught that gratitude opens the heart.

The next thing I do is take notice if it's on heads or tails. Then I start asking a series of questions to nail down if the coin (or message) is for me or someone else. IS the coin someone? Did I have any thoughts or questions in my head at the moment of the "find"? My internal knowing gives me the answers almost instantaneously. I just "know" the answer or action I'm being guided toward.

Sometimes I don't believe the information so in my head

I'm like "no way, did I get that right?" And bam, there will be another coin (or sign) within seconds. The truth is I used to get a little freaked out when I got what I liked to call "confirmation of confirmation." Sometimes the confirmation would be multiple levels deep—I would have to say out loud, "Ok, I got it!" Over time that has become my normal.

~~~

The wedding weekend was fast approaching. Not surprisingly, on the road trip from New Jersey to Michigan, I started finding coins. Each time I expressed gratitude and began coin questioning. "Are you for me?" "Who are you?" "Is there a message?" I paid attention to if I was asking a question or had a thought at the moment of the find. Nothing came. Crickets. All I heard was empty space. I placed each found coin in the right rear pocket of my jeans. They would be placed in the same pocket each day until I knew their purpose. Part of me was wondering if I had lost my "connection," and the other part of me said to "trust and be patient." So I trusted and was patient.

The day had arrived. My dress pants didn't have a "back right pocket" so they would have to go in the front right pocket. I picked up the coins and looked at them in my hand. I don't remember the combination of coins, but I do know they added up to twenty-seven cents—the hard way. It wasn't a quarter and two pennies—it was some other combination. "Twenty-seven" I said to myself, "twenty-seven. OH MY GOD!" I shouted as tears ran down my face.

~~~

Numerology and angel numbers are a study all in themselves. There are plenty of websites and books to check out for yourself. Some are good, some are not so good, and some fall somewhere in the middle. Use your own intuition to find websites and/or books that feel right to you. Understand that I don't claim to be a numerology expert, but I do know enough to get the information I seek. One of the things that I've learned is to reduce whatever pattern of numbers you have down to a single number by adding them together. If you add numbers together and they're still more than one digit, add them again. Keep adding them together until you have a single digit. That single digit is your message.

~~~

"Twenty-seven reduces to NINE!" I exclaimed. "These coins are for the grooms! "NINE is the number of completion. WISH FULFILLED! Now what? Do I make this presentation part of the ceremony OR do I just present it to them?" I opted for the latter.

The ceremony was perfect, and everything went wonderfully. It was even blessed with a light rain during the Apache Blessing. A pride-filled rainbow followed.

During dinner I approached the newlyweds. I spread the coins in front of them as I explained how I work with coins (and spirit). "These are yours" I said. "I started collecting them on my trip out here. Put them with your wedding things to help remember this special day." I explained how, when added together, they equal NINE and that nine represents completion or wish fulfilled. Not surprisingly, my cousins told me they've been together for nine years.

I told my cousins how sometimes after finding a bunch of coins, I'll say: "Thanks. How about coming through with some paper money now?" and then I DO find paper money! They heard the story about the fifty-cent piece in the mail. We shared a moment about his nana (my Aunt Mary) and the stash of candy she also kept in her refrigerator—a reward for having to listen to a story or two that you'd likely heard plenty of times already. We laughed and reflected on times gone by. In that moment we both silently felt her presence. The confirmation would come when I arrived safely back home in New Jersey.

There it was—the stack of mail that accumulated while I was gone. I sorted through it quickly: bill, recycle, recycle, bill. Then, OH MY GOD! Through the window of the envelope a brand new, crisp, one-dollar bill—from the tiger rescue. I carefully opened the envelope and examined the bill, looking for a number or pattern of numbers. There was none. I scanned the rest of the envelope's contents. There it was at the bottom of the letter. A clear sign of who was at the wedding and oh so proud of her grandson and her niece. The letter was signed by none other than Mary Lynn. Following the patterns and exercising patience, I thought the picture was complete. I humbly expressed gratitude.

What happened next made me laugh out loud. I learned another lesson. *I* don't get to decide when something's done. There's clearly a higher force at work. At the end of the day (when I finished writing this story), I emptied my back right pocket. I fished out twenty-seven cents—the easy way, a quarter and two pennies. It was then that I realized *my* wish was also fulfilled on my cousin's wedding day. I was able to escort someone very special to me down the aisle AND stand with him as *his* dream came true!

And I am grateful.

Chapter 7
Hell No!

"HELLLLLLL NO!" The words inside my head resounded so loudly that I looked around to see if anyone else heard them. There was a lot going on in that moment. It seemed as though my brain, my gut, and my heart were all fighting to be heard. A feeling of intense guilt permeated my every cell. I was shocked at how quickly and loudly the words surfaced. Did anyone else hear them? Where the heck did they come from? Who said it? And why? What do I *do* with this information? And who can I even talk to about this? *Who*?

A close and dear co-worker had announced that she was going to donate one of her kidneys to an elderly sibling. The sibling had been on a transplant list but it wasn't looking good; she needed a kidney sooner rather than later. I remembered thinking that offering one of your own organs went way beyond generous. I couldn't even come up with a word or words for how the gesture made me feel—and it wasn't even my sibling or kidney.

As I thought about the procedure and the recovery, the risks and rewards and possible complications, my mind naturally drifted to "what I would do?" My first thoughts were if I could ever donate a part of me that I was still using and could I even imagine what that might feel like. My initial answer was that it would depend. It would depend on what was needed, who needed it, and how old they were. The next thought was barely formed in my head before the HELLLLLL NO erupted from deep within me. It was guttural and came up and out with such force it was like projectile vomit. The thought was whether I would donate to MY sibling, and HELLLLLLLL NO!! was the response.

It was late 2005, nearly three and a half years since our dad had passed rather unexpectedly. My sibling was not maintaining or making proper repairs to our dad's home—the home "left" to both of us. The home where my sibling lived (and raised two children)—*for FREE for almost fifty years* at that point—but that wasn't it. The HELLLLLL NO!! response, a very loud and clear sign, would just need to be filed for now.

The next "sign" was equally eye-opening. My sibling was on a gurney about to be wheeled in for a cardiac procedure. I was present as were my sibling's two adult children. My thoughts danced around, ranging from knowing that both of our parents died suddenly and unexpectedly with heart related issues to the possibility that something could go wrong and that my sibling *might* suffer a similar fate to do I feel a burning desire to say anything that's never been said if something *does* go terribly wrong? Do I need to say "I love you" or "good luck" or "I'm here for you"? A voice inside my head replied quickly, "Nope." Slightly rattled by my response, I internally asked myself the next question: "If this is 'it,' and I don't say anything, will I feel bad or guilty for *not* saying something?" Again, almost immediately came the "nope." Slightly shocked by the calm, matter-of-fact response, I asked myself one last question: "Then why am I here?" "You're *here* for the 'kids' you've always been there for. The 'kids' you've loved like your own, which makes sense." I reasoned with myself and filed away another "sign" that my relationship with my sibling wasn't "normal" but didn't yet understand why.

Cycling back, there were other times when things felt "off" with my sibling's behavior and response to events. There was the time one of my niblings, then five years old, peed their pants at a picnic a few minutes from home. Rather than being a loving, caring parent helping to dry their tears (and then taking them home to get cleaned up), my sibling chose to be selfish, dismissive, and emotionally disconnected from the child's predicament. There was an attitude of "you made the mess—now deal with it." I remember being totally disgusted by my sibling's attitude and behavior. I did right by the child. I told them that "accidents happen, no big deal. I'll take you home to get cleaned up." And that's what I did.

The inappropriate behavior didn't end with my sibling's children; eventually, it extended to the grandchildren as well. Thankfully, there were no "overnights," only a few hours here and there while others were around. My sibling took great pleasure in their fears and discomfort. The grandchildren—twins—were incredibly shy. When they were toddlers they were especially fearful of my sibling's golden retriever. The dog was beautiful but lacked proper training, socialization, and table manners. As such, the twins were outwardly terrified at these visits, and rightfully so. My sibling was amused as the twins tried to stay away from the dog. There was even more amusement as the dog stole food from the kids' plates as they sat frozen with fear while their grandparent laughed. I left my own seat at the "adult" table and got between the dog and the kids so they could enjoy the rest of their meals feeling safe. I could tell by the glaring looks that my sibling hated how I protected the grandchildren; watching them frozen in fear provided better entertainment than the care and concern I provided.

Sadly, there are many more stories of downright evil involving others tangled in my sibling's web—stories that involved cousins, co-workers, friends, animals, in-laws, and romantic interests. There seemed to be just enough fake "nice" sprinkled in to keep the game going, to keep up the facade. Their stories aren't mine to tell, figure out, or heal from, but the patterns of my sibling and how that affected me are.

My sibling's adult children would insist how much my sibling loved me but my internal guidance system said otherwise. I continued to watch, listen, and learn. It became increasingly difficult to spend time around my family of origin, and I couldn't explain why—until I could. My gut was right all along. The first and worst of my abusers was my sibling.

Through the years I had gone to a few different therapists on and off to work through some of my life challenges. The intake process was pretty standard: parents, siblings, grandparents—dead or alive, still married, or divorced. Then they would drill down a little further: jail, drugs, or alcohol abuse. What's your parents' relationship like? What's yours like with them? You get the picture. They *all* missed the sibling abuse. In hindsight, all the therapists were probably just one or two questions away from the *real* taproot of nearly all my internal struggles.

The more time I spent around emotionally healthy people, the less comfortable I felt around my birth family. I couldn't put words to it and didn't fully understand why. Gatherings and holidays felt fake. I attended out of obligation and to see my sibling's grandchildren, the littles I adored and did my best to protect.

I was at a family picnic playing badminton after recently having Lasik eye surgery. My sibling's reaction to me nearly taking the birdie in the eyes struck a nerve deep inside me. The reaction of complete amusement caused my sibling to lift up a leg to prevent bladder leakage. I saw the sickening smile despite a quick turn to try and hide how amused my near miss reaction made them. It disgusted me.

I wanted to scream, cry, and run away all at the same time. I could feel my insides churning and my face becoming flushed. In that moment I felt I had very few options. If I expressed myself, I would be mocked. If I left, my sibling would have won. So I did what I always did: I sucked it up and continued playing despite my hidden emotional tidal waves. We finished the game. I maintained a healthy distance until I felt I could leave without my sibling thinking they hurt me. Stifling emotions was my own unhealthy pattern. Truth be told, it was a survival skill I learned at a very young age.

On the drive home I called a friend who met me at my house. She patiently listened as I tearfully told her what had happened. I spoke of how the amused body language of my sibling affected me on a level I had no words for. My internal response felt stronger than my brain's logic. Was I overreacting? Losing my mind?

When I finished and was temporarily all cried out, my friend asked two questions: Had I ever felt like "this" before?

Without hesitation, I said, "Yes, lots of times."

"Will you tell me about that?" she said.

I told story after story about fabricated lies my sibling told our mother that would get me a good beating, no questions asked. My sibling would watch me get the daylights smacked out of me, all the while standing behind our mother laughing, pointing, and mocking me as I cried and begged our mother to stop. When I ran out of stories, my friend took a deep breath and asked me one last question.

"Have you ever heard of sibling abuse?"

Chapter 8
Sibling Abuse

"Sibling abuse?" I repeated. "What are you talking about? There's no such thing. There's sibling rivalry, kids will be kids," and I trailed off.

There was a deafening silence between us as I tried to understand those two simple words. Eventually, I broke the silence.

"Wait, how did my therapists *miss* this? How did they miss something SO BIG? And how do I tell my sibling's adult children that not just one but BOTH of their parents abused me?"

My friend explained that in healthy families a normal amount of taunting and teasing occurs between siblings and/or other family members. However, when it is frequent, extreme, or crosses the line, it is abuse. She suggested I start healing myself by making an appointment with my latest therapist and reading the book entitled *Sibling Abuse* by Vernon R. Wiehe. I did both.

When I cracked open that book my memory and emotional floodgates burst open. I felt like I was alone in a paper boat rushing downstream in a storm without a life jacket or a paddle. I cycled between flashbacks, "aha" moments, extreme sadness, justifiable anger, frustration, disappointment, disbelief, and relief. I spent the next several months reading, journaling, and trying to make sense of it all. I had five months to come to terms with all of this, five months until the family member I was closest to would be in town, five months until we could have a very difficult in-person conversation.

As I turned the pages of *Sibling Abuse,* I recalled the earliest memory. As a toddler I shared a room with my sibling. Soon after "lights out" my sibling would regularly beg me to climb out of my crib and come to their bed. I was held tightly in a bear hold as they yelled to our mother, "MA! Sherri's in my bed!" My mother returned me to my bed with a scolding. The scene played out multiple times as I trusted my sibling's repeated promises not to yell for our mother as her scolding escalated to beatings. Eventually, I would cry myself to sleep while my sibling snickered beneath the bed covers

In a later memory I was age eleven. My sibling and their spouse fed me alcohol during a New Year's Eve party to the point where I became falling down drunk. There were other "adults" present, including one of my cousins. I was the only one who was not at least eighteen. While all this was going on, my sibling's five-month-old baby slept in the next room. The scene didn't end there. They stripped me naked, threw me into the bathtub, and forced me to drink black coffee as they laughed and snapped pictures.

They laughed again the next morning while telling me how I foamed at the mouth once I passed out. They laughed for days without concern or remorse about how much worse that night could have been. Their actions could have killed me.

If you grew up with a sibling like mine, you already know there were many more incidents besides the two I described. Yes, there is a normal amount of teasing that occurs between siblings. However, what I repeatedly experienced was a disgusting abuse of power considering the seven-year age difference. Imagine paging through the ages. What chance does a two-year-old have against a nine-year-old, an eleven-year-old against an eighteen-year-old?

Events that I had completely normalized now had a different glow. It is NOT remotely close to normal to be purposefully and frequently kicked, scratched, pinched, bitten, spit on, tied up, locked in a closet, bedroom, or dark basement, held under water, shoved, tripped, have your hair pulled, tickled until you cry, squeezed between someone's thighs like a vise, called names that have been permanently banished from the dictionary, incessantly mocked for any reason, or made to frequently beg for mercy like a dog while on your knees with your hands clasped in front of your heart. This is NOT normal behavior between siblings on *any* day. Yet, it was considered "normal" for me. This revelation found my thoughts bouncing around like the balls in a bingo machine.

Those first five months were tough. I did not interact with my sibling at all and was a "no show" for Thanksgiving and Christmas dinners with "the family." Repressed emotions surfaced like the burnt coating on the bottom of a stock pot angrily scraped off by a metal spatula. These are deep wounds that may never scab over or completely heal. I struggled to find someone to see and hear me. The therapists missed it. My closest friends at that time were also incapable of grasping the gravity of my childhood traumas. They couldn't understand how the abuse I suffered affected every single part of my adult life and relationships.

I desperately wanted and needed someone to be there to listen, to understand, and to see the little girl inside of me who was still wounded from being treated so terribly—someone who could help me navigate telling the family and "next steps" for healing. What I received were comments like "that was so long ago—let it go," "you should go on medication," "it wasn't that bad," "maybe they were abused, too," and "forgive and forget." These statements didn't feel good at all. They made me feel as if my feelings were somehow bad or wrong. The words also made excuses for my abuser(s). I felt hurt, violated, isolated, and alone.

It was like being abused all over again.

Some nights I hardly slept, and some nights I would sleep fitfully. Many times I woke with a salty crust around my eyes from crying in my sleep. The shaky, fearful, little voice inside my head was getting louder.

Speak your truth. It will set you free.

Chapter 9
The Tell

The five months I had to prepare myself for that difficult conversation went by quickly and slowly at the same time. During my entire adult life I was asked variations of the same question by so many people, all with the same intonation of disbelief, "Wait, you two are related?" I also lost track of how many times my sibling's own adult children asked us both, "Why don't you two get along?" My sibling would shrug their shoulders and make a cutesy face while I found myself without words or a good explanation. Until now.

It doesn't feel good to talk poorly about someone, especially your own family member. But it also doesn't feel good to keep secrets to the detriment of your own emotional health and physical well-being. The truth is there are some really messed up people in this world, and they all belong to someone—they *all* have a family of origin. The reported numbers of abuse are staggering enough, let alone wondering how much goes *UNreported* because of fear not only perpetuates the problem but exacerbates it.

I repeatedly ask my spirit guides for signs and guidance when I write the difficult chapters. "Do I need to put them in the book?" I would ask. "Can I write about the wonderful gifts I have without explaining where they came from?" Over a six-week span of time, I asked the question or had thoughts regarding the hard chapters. Most of the time I would get my answer in coins. Every day for over six weeks, walking pretty much the same way, I'd find coins—a crazy number of coins. This is not a book on numerology, but suffice it to say I was receiving a tremendous amount of divine encouragement and support. In addition to the coins, I bumped into people I hadn't seen in years, and they would open up to me about their *own* stories of abuse

~~~

It's here. The day is here. My family of origin communicated through yelling, sarcasm, the silent treatment, and manipulating someone else do the talking for them. Little did I know then that I was about to chart a new course for myself *and* my future. My intention was to speak kindly, clearly, and courageously.

"I'm so sorry. I feel horrible telling you like this," I began while driving the family member (not my sibling) I felt the most connected with to Newark Airport in the wee hours of January 2, 2017. "I hoped to tell you sooner. We were supposed to have dinner just the two of us. That never happened, and now you're going back and I just can't hold it in anymore. I've been holding it in for almost five months already. It sucks unloading this, and you're about to board a plane with a bunch of strangers." Through tears I blurted out the awful truth about my sibling. It was gut-wrenching.

Keeping quiet did nothing for my healing but verbally vomiting the ugly truth about my sibling to their adult child before they boarded a plane didn't feel so great either. I apologized profusely for the terrible timing and acknowledged how difficult this information must be to hear. As we said goodbye at departing flights, I gave my full support for *their* well-being. "Talk to whoever you need to about this. Please don't worry about betraying my trust. I'm not keeping this secret. I also know this information affects you, too. I'm very sorry I had to tell you this way, boarding a plane with a bunch of strangers. I love you." I pulled away when I could no longer see them.

It's all out there. Now what?

Chapter 10

After the Tell

It didn't take long to receive the first text after the pre-dawn data dump on the way to "departing flights" regarding my older sibling. "I'm here and remember you can always talk to me. I just need to understand this before I can even discuss this with anyone. Thank you for being able to tell me."

Three days later I received another text to the effect of "I won't be telling anyone. This is your story to tell. If you want the relationship that I have with my sibling, hopefully you two will go to counseling to work through this. We should probably discuss this over the phone at some point."

A few hours later another text arrived: "I have fully digested what you have told me. I'm not sure what you expected me to do other than listen and be there for you, which I have done and will continue to do."

~~~

Five months wasn't nearly enough time for *me* to digest being repeatedly tortured and abused by my own sibling. I'm really not sure how anyone could have possibly done it in ***three days!*** Heck, I'm five years out, and I'm *still* learning and healing! I answered the lifelong question of why my sibling and I don't get along. Yet, the first family member I told, the one I felt the most connected to, didn't like the answer. I suspect they didn't like the answer because it meant that not one but both ***their*** parents repeatedly abused me. What does one do with *that* information?

~~~

Eventually, that first family member did tell their sibling who reached out to let me know they knew. They also said that *my* sibling "knows what you're saying about them and they said they were abused, too." I laughed and asked, "By whom? It sure sounds more like a convenient excuse to me since THEY were *my* abuser!" I never did get an answer. They said they'd figure out a way for me to continue being included in things and that they didn't want it to affect my relationship with three little ones I protected from another family member who repeatedly molested little girls—including me and his own sister.

In the beginning I had so much hope that they would stay true to their word, that they would figure out a way for me to be included to see the little ones at least. Picture after picture from events I was deliberately kept away from were posted on social media. I called to ask where my invitation was and was told my sibling was there so I could come the next day "for leftovers." "No thanks, you can shove your leftovers." After blocking the first two people to protect my emotional well-being, I was accused of being angry. Not one of them understood the depth of my hurt. Their lack of inclusion felt like I was being abused all over again.

I tried being patient with their process. After all, it's not every day someone tells you that they were repeatedly abused by not one but both of *their* parents. There was even a part of me that thought maybe for once my sibling would be the one to take the high road—you know, be accountable by apologizing and taking corrective action for the sake of the family. Nope. I'm fairly certain they were waiting for me to take action and come crawling back begging like I always did.

Nope. Not again. Not *this* time.

Time marched on. Remember that family member I took to

the airport? The one who thanked me for telling them and said they would continue to be there for me? A very strange sequence of events happened that left me finding out completely by accident that they were in town for Easter week. When I called to inquire about why we didn't get together like usual, I was harshly accused of stalking them. I explained how the information made its way to me and then asked if they had time to see my abuser. Their answer was undeniable proof that they deliberately avoided me and, despite claims to be neutral, their actions proved otherwise. It was the last time I was going to feel like I had been kicked off the couch by a family member. That person's actions pushed me into grieving the loss of my entire living family. It is a terribly painful and isolating experience I wouldn't wish on anyone.

~~~

"Don't do it, don't do it. Hang on, just hang on. It will be better tomorrow. Those bastards will get everything you've worked so hard for. They don't deserve it, you can't let them win. Take back your power!" Those words from deep inside of me kept me going. I didn't know where they came from, and at that time I didn't really care either. I was struggling on the outside, struggling on the inside, wanted to sleep the pain away but couldn't, and found very little joy in anything while I was awake. At that time only one person was aware of how dangerously close I came to extinguishing my own light—only one, the one who gave my abuse its name, the one I will forever be grateful to.

During a brief moment of mental clarity, I knew I had to update my will and beneficiaries. I also knew I didn't really have the emotional bandwidth to do it. That little voice kept me going while I dove into the subject matter of childhood abuse. I learned about ACE (Adverse Childhood Experience) scores, repressed emotions and memories, PTSD, the wounded inner child (ren), triggers, re-parenting myself, cellular memory, and so much more.

It was by far the scariest and darkest time of my entire life.

I was afraid for myself.

It took an enormous amount of effort to do even the simplest of tasks. Sometimes I wouldn't eat. Sometimes I wouldn't shower for days. If you read my first book, you already know how some days the only time I left the house was to check on a friend's dogs. The love of those dogs helped keep me alive. Eventually, I had to find a way to dig myself out. I knew I needed distractions so I had to trick myself with deadlines and rewards. For instance, I knew I wanted to buy a motorcycle despite not having a clue how to even start one, much less ride one. I signed up to take a safety class first. As my emotional fog began to lift, I knew I had to get my beneficiaries and will in order ***first.*** I booked the motorcycle class, which gave me a hard deadline to get the will done, and I follow through.

The next extreme (for a fifty-something-year-old) thing that I did was sign up to be a whitewater river guide. If standing arm in arm in the middle of Lehigh River rapids with a bunch of strangers didn't distract me, nothing would. Not only did I purposefully work to overcome the intense fear of water my sibling was responsible for, but I began to trust again, AND I started to build myself a new family—a river family.

In time I would come to understand who the voice was and what she needed. It was the voice of one of my wounded inner children. This one was my wounded teenager. She's incredibly sassy and fearless. Hers is an attitude of "let me drive for a while, I'll show you how to do it"—and then DOES! I have come to really love and appreciate her presence in my life! She has a powerful voice and gets things done. I believe she has been in the driver's seat for the better part of my adult life. She's also the one who challenged some of the crap lines I was fed growing up. Bullshit sayings like "Family is everything, and blood is thicker than water." She was also the one who saw hell freezing over and pigs flying at the thought of her older sibling stepping up and being accountable. Counseling with me? That thought brought the kind of sustained, audible laughter that makes your stomach hurt.

My inner teenager had the reins. I heard her ask, "If we have to start building a new family, maybe we should try dating? What's the worst thing that could happen?"

Chapter 11
Smack

SMACK! She slapped me across the face, from behind, unprovoked, in the presence of two of my closest friends. The sound and tingling sensation in my face thrust me back to childhood, back to the beatings I received from an angry mother who believed every word of a sociopathic, narcissistic, older sibling. Instantly, my experience seemed to split, just like a fork in the road. I was momentarily in two places at once. In one frame I could see my younger wounded inner child receiving another undeserved beating; helpless, hopeless, alone, fearful, and completely overpowered. In the second frame I was an adult woman who had worked through many of the lifetime fears and limitations dumped onto me by others.

In that moment time froze. It was as if someone pressed the pause button so I could decide which road to take and how to respond instead of react. I quickly processed what had happened; the conversation leading up to the slap, the slap, the velocity and force of its delivery, and the awful sound made when her rage-filled hand connected with the left side of my face. I further considered the looks of shock and disbelief on the faces of both of my friends, confirming that something completely horrifying had, in fact, happened. Their expressions affirmed what I felt and knew to be true: My girlfriend of nearly four years had completely crossed the line.

~~~

The four of us were on our way to meet others at a stable in North Jersey for a horseback riding excursion in honor of my recent birthday. I was riding shotgun, with my then girlfriend behind me and my other two friends seated on the left side of the truck. We were on our way to an adventure so the mood was fun and lighthearted. We approached the infamous Somerville circle, talking and laughing about Jersey drivers.

My friend who was driving remarked how people had changed since being required to wear a mask due to COVID. "It's crazy," she said. "People have forgotten how to use their arms now that they have to wear a mask."

When the laughter subsided, I added, "Yeah, just like those people that have to turn the radio down when they're backing into a driveway."

And that's when it happened.

SMACK! Completely out of nowhere, and with an incredible amount of anger and accuracy, the slap was delivered to the left side of my face. I was unjustifiably and quite shockingly struck from behind—by someone who often talked about taking our relationship to the next level.

The ferocious force rang my bell and sent a familiar tingle of alarm through my entire body. Anyone who has experienced severe childhood beatings knows what I speak of. It is an unnatural feeling that swiftly washes over every cell of your body. It begins at the point of impact.

As I attempted to turn around to face my assaulter, I couldn't help but notice the horrified look on both of my friends' faces. I stopped just short of turning all the way around. I really didn't want to face such hostility and ugliness but I also didn't want to succumb to it. My friends looked to me for guidance on how to proceed. Uncomfortable doesn't adequately describe the moment.

I quickly weighed my options. I chose the "right" side of the fork in the road. I *chose* to respond rather than react. "What the heck was that?" I asked, already knowing that no answer could possibly justify being hit.

Her response was, "I didn't mean to hit you that hard!"

"That hard? You shouldn't be hitting me at all. You crossed the line."

The silence that followed was incredibly eerie. Since I was the guest of honor and carrying the balance of the group's money, I had no choice. We *had* to show up. There was no way we could just dump her on the side of the road. She had a key to my house after all—no telling what she might do there, unsupervised, out of anger.

~~~

One of the "gifts" of being a multiple abuse survivor is the ability to squash, stifle, or hide how I'm really feeling. It is a learned trauma response that kept me "safe" from ridicule "compliments" of the repeated sibling abuse. I neatly tucked my present emotions away and was determined to have a good time celebrating my birthday with friends—and did.

The truth is I had either completely dismissed or minimized earlier signs. Growing up the way I did, I flip-flopped between being too tolerant and making excuses for others' behavior. *This* event was the universe's way of making sure I finally got the message. Who does that? Who tries to "slap the happy" out of someone? In time the insidiousness of it all would actually make me laugh. I am so grateful it *only* took four years to figure out.

~~~

We first began talking on an online dating site. I honestly don't remember who initiated the contact, and it doesn't much matter now anyway. Our dating profiles lined up nicely, and we had enough common interests to schedule a "meet" despite living nearly two hours apart. The first sign, obvious now but subtle then, was that her main profile picture was just that: a profile. She was only letting me see one side, her "best" side, her "light" side. The "shady" side—her dark, unhealed, angry side—was completely hidden from view.

~~~

Jim Thorpe, Pennsylvania, was a little north of halfway, but she agreed to meet me there after river guide training one spring Saturday in 2017. An electronics/detail junkie by nature, her research of the area uncovered plenty of shopping opportunities to pass the time waiting for my arrival. It was a very busy, public place, and safe for both of us.

"Just so you know I consider this a 'meet,' not a date. I'm in town for the weekend for training, and I'm staying in a room above the restaurant. I'm not looking for a hookup and don't plan to ask you to spend the night. That's just not how I roll," I explained right up front.

Our meals were identical, right down to the salad dressing and how we liked our steaks cooked. The conversation was light and easy. We felt comfortable enough to compare notes about some of the others on the dating site, noting that "this one's looking for a hookup, that one wants a threesome, and this one's partner wants to watch, and oh my gods—watch out for this one!" We had a nice dinner, walked around some, and ended the night with an appropriate-length first hug.

I was busy with guide training, and she was busy maintaining her "too large for one person" property—mowing her lawn, picking up sticks, and caring for a pool that she would only use if others were there. Occasionally, she would talk of playing golf with a friend and how she didn't like a particular golf course or some of the other people she played with. She didn't seem to have the kind of active friendships I had with my friends. *To each his own,* I thought. *Everybody's different.*

My internal radar went off with how soon after that first meet that she invited me to her house for an overnight and how quickly she spoke of "our long-range plan."

"I have a spare bedroom with its own half bath," she said.

I wasn't sure then if my alarm sounded because it really **was** too soon or because of my own trust triggers or if my guidance system was alerting me that her actions weren't lining up with her words. Understandably, it was really hard for me to trust anybody, even myself sometimes. We talked about "going slow, and friends first." Yet, I was being asked to stay overnight—with someone I hardly knew. I told myself that I was safe and always had choices. *Time would tell.*

We met in Jim Thorpe or New Hope every couple of weeks and spent the day together. September brought our birthdays, one week apart, mine first. I made my own plans to attend a women's weekend spiritual retreat. (My inner teenager wanted new experiences.) The day before my birthday/retreat, she kept asking if my mail arrived. I assured her I'd let her know. I was told to wait and open it while she was on the phone.

She was very thoughtful in her gift giving that first birthday. It took effort to research how to make homemade beef jerky and borrow the tools needed. She also had a necklace made with three charms that represented who I am.

The woman I was learning about also made her own birthday plans that year. She rented a rustic cabin near Raystown Lake and invited me to come along. I agreed to join her for the better part of it. We used part of that trip to plan our next trip two months later. For the most part, she and I traveled well and took some really amazing trips together. In between those two trips I felt comfortable enough to see where and how she lived.

Her house and property were very nice but way more than I would want to maintain, especially with the active lifestyle I enjoyed. It was better suited for a young couple with kids. Since she still worked full time, it would take multiple days in the summer just to mow the lawn and care for the pool, then there were the inside chores. If it rained she'd get herself all worked up over when the grass would get cut. She had an attitude of "What would the neighbors think?" *This* was another subtle sign that I completely dismissed. Surely, there were signs along the way. I had to start asking myself some hard questions.

Is love really that blind? How did it get to this? What did I do wrong? How did I get here? What's *MY* part in all of it? What led up to getting smacked? What vibe am I giving off that makes people think it's OK to abuse me? There's got to be more!

Chapter 12

After the Smack

As I was getting to know the woman I met online, I was also starting to *really* get to know myself. I began feeling emotions, processing memories, and learning about healthy childhood development, coping skills, co-dependency, triggers, *and* dysfunction. I remember the unhealed parts of me being inwardly annoyed and pissed off with the notion of "re-parenting myself," realizing that I had to go backwards and re-live some of the horror before I could move forward. It felt as if my life choices at that time were sucky and suckier. But at least I had someone who thought I was worth it, someone who began to hate my birth family as much as I did, then finally someone on my side who actually agreed with me!

Despite outwardly displaying a confident, capable, independent persona to the world growing up, I struggled inwardly to believe any of it. At times others would jokingly describe me as being "wound too tight." Many times facts rest in jest. The truth is I was! At work I smiled under the worst of circumstances, saying to myself, *Fake it till you make it.* And make it I did!

My journey to heal from childhood abuse has not been as simple, loving, and gentle as the picture of "peeling the layers off an onion" that the therapists have painted. It's been more like running said onion mercilessly over a metal cheese grater—on the side with the biggest holes. *This, too, shall pass* is another incomplete BS phrase. The truth is sometimes it'll pass with the grace of a kidney stone!

~~~

I was in a weird place. It felt like I was watching a circus from above as I struggled to balance on the high wire. Some days I felt the repressed emotions rise slowly and dramatically like a velvet curtain at the start of a show. Other days they flung themselves out forcefully like a lion's roar. Once exposed, the emotions spun like plates in the air. I paid close attention to which one needed attention that day and which I should let crash to the floor. There were still other days when I felt as if I was the floor of an elephant's cage—cold, hard, and damp, a dumping ground for others' waste. Ironically, I was an honorary ringmaster when the circus came to my small town *before* the curtain rose on the sibling abuse. I started to understand that what I grew up thinking was normal was anything but.

The parents who were supposed to love and protect me hadn't. Not because they were bad people but because they lacked the skills to be good parents. My older sibling, the person I looked up to and tried to emulate as a youngster, I began to see very, very differently. With the stage lights turned up, I now saw the worst kind of ugly—a manipulative, narcissistic, sociopath who fed off other people's pain. I realized that what was supposed to be the longest and closest relationship of my life was instead the most toxic. I grew up with so many screwy beliefs about life and how things work that I was astonished how I had managed to function and be successful in the world at all!

I started working through my pain piece by piece, trigger by trigger, fear by fear, pattern by pattern, and belief by belief. Some pieces still fit; some got tossed. The same was true for the triggers, fears, patterns, and beliefs. In time I would come to understand that I lived much of my life in fight or flight (also known as survival) mode. The conditioning I received *was* directly attributed to my older sibling and disconnected parents. As a toddler, I couldn't just pack up my stuff and leave. Looking back, I was stuck and know I had no choices *then.*

The first and hardest step was forgiving me. I did *not* live life in denial. I truly did not know what I did not know. The second step was to work through the shame of feeling stupid for taking so long *to* know. Third, I had to be gentle with myself in the process. It was extremely important to celebrate my successes, however small.

The truth is:

I

AM

AMAZING.

I am even MORE amazing considering all I endured. Lastly, I had to "own" where I was and where I was headed.

Looking back, I learned that my life models for relationships, communication, conflict resolution, boundaries, and so many other life skills were defective. My parents and grandparents were both divorced; no relationship experts there. My sibling graduated high school, married, turned age eighteen, and welcomed their first child to the world all in three months, and— except for a few months span of time—*never* moved out of our dad's house. The communication skills I observed were yelling, sarcasm, and the silent treatment. Conflicts were never really resolved; the stronger one was just given in to. Dad's famous words were always: "But, Sher, that's your sibling." Those words subliminally indicated I had to "take the high road and give in." Personal and physical boundaries were also nonexistent. Since I was "the baby," I had to quietly take what was dished and like it. I remember several instances when I was very young—minding my own business, playing alone, and without warning or provocation—being grabbed by my ponytail and dragged into the house for an undeserved beating while my sibling stood by laughing. They knew full well they were the instigator. As an adult, I keep my hair super short and spiked, knowing full well it's an unhealed childhood trauma strategy that reduces my internal struggle of having it pulled by anyone ever again.

~~~

I know now I was a good kid, but in those moments I didn't understand what was going on and believed I somehow deserved what I got. At no point growing up was I told or shown that I had any choices. Not once. I remember vividly being told (by my mother) when going to someone's house, "Don't you dare ask them for anything." I can still feel the shaking fear "younger Sherri" felt. My family of origin served as a bad example for so many of the things that caused me pain in my adult life. Sadly, it took me over fifty years to see it—fifty years to start to be able to do my life differently.

Growing up in chaos was normal; so juggling multiple things while initially trying to heal was normal, too. For me, focusing on just one thing at a time probably wouldn't have provided enough respite. That said, I was simultaneously grieving the loss of my entire living family and the potential for what could have been, learning about dysfunction and childhood abuse and how to heal from it, actively training as a river guide to overcome my fear of water, learning how to ride a motorcycle, starting to date again, seeing clients, trying to build a new life/family for myself, playing softball, and maintaining a house. Good thing I retired at age forty-eight from full-time work! Being that busy also assured me more frequent nights of restful, restorative sleep.

~~~

As I started to develop confidence and discernment, I also found my voice. I had begun challenging what others were saying that didn't feel right to me. For instance, I remember different therapists asking if I wanted to "play the victim for the rest of my life," implying that I was not a victim. That statement echoed in my head for a very long time especially knowing I had heard similar versions of it multiple times. The truth, *MY* truth, is that I absolutely *WAS* a victim. Growing up where and how I did was NOT a choice for me. To make my truth any less than that is belittling and simply not OK. Now that I know differently, I DO have a choice, and I have chosen to be a victor!

There was another statement that took a while for me to process. This one was made by one of my sibling's adult children months after the sibling abuse conversation. The statement was something to the effect of me "blaming their parent (my sibling) for everything." The "family way" would have been to just shout back, "Well, they are!" Instead, I held my tongue. I did not respond quickly and harshly; I contemplated many of the different fears and beliefs that I had. I recalled specific events that connected the fears to my sibling *and* several instances of the name-calling for the unwarranted beliefs. The list was long. My sibling **was** undeniably to blame for my fear of the dark, my fear of being restrained, my fear of the water, my fear of being alone, my fear of expressing my emotions, my believing that everyone thought I was a cheater and a liar, and feeling stupid, ugly, unworthy, and unlovable. I also realized that what I knew to be true is extremely hard for others to swallow. I've worked through all the fears and know that the beliefs are not mine to carry. The beliefs belong to my sibling. My sibling is the kind of ugly I will never be.

~~~

Sorting through all of this took time and effort. I deserved all the "downtime" I took for myself. I filled myself with energy work, body work, time in nature, and whatever felt good at the time. I read and learned and healed and grew.

Others walking a similar path began finding their way to me, and we learned from each other. I even started learning how to set boundaries. It felt so good to be able to speak my truth and ask for what I needed—even when it made others uncomfortable. I began to see the light and some very promising signs at the end of the tunnel. I slowed things down and learned to decide if my gut was giving me proper warnings or if I was responding to being triggered. I listened to other people's crazy much less and started trusting myself a lot more!

I realized I owed it to myself to take an honest look back at the last four years to see what patterns or behaviors I might have missed, minimized, or normalized. Truthfully, the "smack" wasn't the first time her anger was directed at me. But it *was* the last.

Chapter 13
Chasing Crazy

Filled with a fiery anger, she got up into my face as she stood toe-to-toe with me. Her whole essence emanated a familiar rage. Rigid body. Fixed eyes. They blazed into me with the crazed look of a rabid animal. I felt the heat from her breath as she viciously shouted at me through gritted teeth and a clenched jaw, "YOU BETTER MANIFEST THAT ALL THIS STUFF FITS INTO TWO STORAGE UNITS!"

I stood there.

I stood there with compassion. For myself, for her, and for the situation. She was moving. Strangers were in the house she'd lived in for many, many years—by herself, with a partner, then by herself again. These strangers were not only traipsing all over her personal space but they were also touching her stuff and hauling it into the moving truck. They were relocating it into storage units because she hadn't bought a new house yet. Her immediate plan was to live in her sister's basement until she could find a place that checked all her boxes—an incredibly tall order for someone as particular as she. A control freak by nature, this self-inflicted situation clearly pushed every single one of her buttons. Unable to self-regulate, she chose to unleash her fury on me. And I took it.

She stood there.

I stood there.

It was momentary but felt like forever. In that space,

without me adding any fuel, her crazed anger was stifled. I responded rather than retorting with equal intensity. "That's not mine to manifest," I finally replied matter-of-factly.

Bewildered, the mercury began to rise again as she said, "Well, the lady at the storage place said it'll all fit—two units is perfect for a three-bedroom house."

Does she not realize just how much stuff she has? That she doesn't "just" have an everyday kind of three-bedroom house?

I drew in a big breath. She was waiting for an answer, and a tall task awaited me.

By this point in our relationship, I had learned much about the woman who stood before me. Like many Virgos (myself included), she doesn't like asking for help, has incredibly strong opinions, and absolutely despises being challenged or wrong— about anything. She angrily demanded that I manifest a mountainous miracle, and I had no choice but to be gentle with the truth—a truth she was completely denying.

As compassionately and gently as I could, I began, "You have more than the standard three-bedroom house." I paused to make sure she was listening and didn't see me as an adversary or threat. "Much more," I continued slowly and deliberately. "For starters, you have stuff in your attic, a full finished basement with an extra room that has more storage behind a curtain and serves as your home gym, a garage, pool shed, potting shed, and an outbuilding for the yard maintenance items that don't fit in your garage. Did you happen to mention any of that to the storage place lady?"

I saw her head was spinning as she processed my words. I paused again before finishing, "You're definitely going to need another unit."

Faced with the undeniable truth and fully frustrated, she stomped away. In some ways I think she felt personally attacked, as though I had silently insinuated she *deliberately* lied to the storage gal. I also believe she resented me for "being right" rather than seeing that I was the only one (besides the paid movers) who were there to help. I began to see me, our relationship, and her through a very different lens. I noticed that the more I accommodated her, the more she wanted and expected.

I began to wonder, *was I chasing crazy?*

Chapter 14
Letting Go of a Friend

I "let go" of a friend today. They came into my life six years ago. The year was 2016. I was involved in so many things back then—so many things that I hoped would help put the "unity" back into my community. There were a lot of people around me at that point, many who shared the vision of restoring our tiny borough to its former glory. The friend I had to let go was a tangible reminder and symbol of the feeling of hope, love, and inclusion I had for my hometown—and secretly for myself.

There was a span of time when different pockets of groups worked diligently to create interesting new events intended to get people off their couch and active in the community. The desire was to reestablish the small-town feel many of us remembered growing up here.

Our art council organized artsy events, the library offered new and exciting programs, and the recreation commission held charity fundraising events, holiday parties, and fun runs. The friend entered my life during the planning and execution of our town's second (and last) annual color run.

A color run is a noncompetitive running event whereby participants are doused with different colored cornstarch at stations set up in areas along the route. Runners typically wear white to accentuate how badly they were "hit" at each stop. Some participants would stay at the back of the pack so they could roll around in the excess color that made its way to the ground. Others would purchase *extra* packets of color to either spread on their face like war paint, add to complete their ensemble, or save for the finish line celebration. No one was safe from the people tasked with applying the color, not even the spectators or innocent passersby!

My friend and I didn't spend much time together while the event was being planned. Our bond began on race day. We were inseparable. I'm not usually one to warm up that quickly, but this was different. Maybe it was the energy and excitement of the event. Maybe it was the feeling of being connected with a higher purpose. Maybe it was the camaraderie. I honestly don't know. But I do know that *this* friend felt warm, close, and supportive. There was an inner sense of pride for what we were doing.

The run day weather was perfect—always a gamble when planning an outdoor event—and everyone had a great time. Once the last runner crossed the finish line, there was a big color celebration as the DJ engaged the crowd. Packets of blue, orange, green, and yellow were tossed into the air. It created a gigantic colorful dust cloud that left no one untouched. Similar to the grand finale of a fireworks display, the color cloud marked the end of the event.

My friend and I left feeling really good about the success of the run. After that we would get together from time to time out in public, but over time our relationship changed. Just like the seasons, it faded. Sometimes my friend would show up for chores. A bleach splash changed the relationship even more. I was forced to cut off the sleeves and stop wearing my friend out in public.

My friend, the black T-shirt with our town's blue and white color run logo on the front and "staff" on the back, was running out of time and fabric. With more holes than a slice of good Swiss cheese, my pal was reserved for sleep and house chores. Week after week I promised myself this was the "last week" or "last wash" until it *really* had to go. My head *knew* it was "just a shirt," but my heart felt so much more. It felt the connections and hope I had for my hometown and so many of the people I'd made memories with. It also represented my personal pattern of holding onto things and people waaaay too long. It was an incredibly bittersweet moment. Through tear-filled eyes and with a tightened throat and heavy heart, I thanked and blessed my friend as I lifted the trash can lid. As I struggled to let my friend go, I heard myself say, "It's just a shirt." Another voice whispered back, "Or is it?"

Chapter 15
Along the Way

My journey has not been linear, and the signs have not always made sense the moment I received them. As you make your way through this book, you will read how sometimes feelings, signs, and messages have taken me decades to process or understand. At other times my interpretation was clouded due to the unhealed, wounded parts of me. As I unraveled my story and healed from the trauma and abuse, the intended messages and wisdom were understood almost instantaneously. I am able to move through the muck so much faster working WITH my guides instead of resisting and fighting what I am being shown.

I struggled for weeks about writing my "next chapter" of this book. The folks in my writers' group wanted to know "what comes next." I had taken a few chapters in one direction with an old girlfriend and left them hanging, then I started another thread with someone else and left my writers' group hanging again. I promised to finish the thought the following week and didn't. The truth is: Some of what I'm writing is painful, and I'm not in a hurry to relive it. I also know that I have to revisit *some* of it to "get" the lessons so they aren't repeated. That said, this chapter is about me being gentle with myself. Life throws curves. We get derailed and sidetracked. I get to change my mind about what I'm doing and when I'm doing it. And so do you!

~~~

I've learned that sometimes the message I receive in coins is not about the total tally so much as the number or patterns of coins and other "signs" along the way. As I write this, I hear different birds singing and chirping, and a lone crow reminds me there's magic everywhere and to tune in (or tune out) and pay attention even if only for a few moments each day. I close my eyes and immerse myself in the moment and listen in a way few do. I feel birds take flight and join them with my imagination. I hear a plane pass overhead and wonder what adventure the passengers are embarking on. A train speeds by in the distance, reminding me of the hurried life so many still live. And I return to writing renewed and rejuvenated, knowing that in all of it, each piece is part of the whole.

~~~

Today was the third day of a pattern taking shape. On day one I found three pennies. On day two I found the same. Three feels warm and makes my heart sing and smile. Three is a very magical and powerful number in its own rite, and for me it also represents three very special young people that I miss terribly. When I get three, I take it as a sign that they are thinking about me, too.

On day three I went about my walk picking up coins and putting them in my front right pocket as I always do when wearing shorts. While drinking my coffee, half paying attention to the total or amount of coins in my pocket, something told me to stop and count. So I did. The coins tallied forty-one. I chuckled. That number was someone's athletic number—someone who was once very special to me. The chuckle came because I knew their birthday was right around the corner. It was also knowing some of the recent patterns of numbers relating to my family of origin. I'd recently found combinations of coins that represented my parents' death ages and years of birth as well as my sibling's year of birth and current age. Signs of the "family" almost always make me chuckle now. The time and distance away from most of them has been good for me, my soul, and my personal healing journey.

This morning's coins were more about the "threes" than any possible message from the total sum. When I laid them out, I laughed out loud. Three dimes, three nickels, and three pennies— three sets of three. "Nine" I said to myself. "Nine is the number of completion, otherwise known as wish fulfilled." I *know* that the universe already knows what's in my heart as it relates to the three "littles" I speak of often, and I'm reminded regularly that they are getting closer to me every single moment.

Today's coins only tell part of the story. I found one of the pennies next to a trash can a crow was picking through. I was only about six feet away when I began conversing with him. I started by thanking him for letting me get so close and then asked if there was anything good in there.

He stopped, turned to face me, looked straight into my soul, and said, "You'd be surprised by what people throw away."

Having experienced being thrown away by my birth family and finding so much value in all the coins people toss away every single day, I laughed and told the crow, "Yeah, don't I know it."

His next message wasn't as audible. In fact, it was barely a whisper, but I still heard it. "Things aren't always what they seem," he said.

"Hmmm," I thought. "Is there more?"

"Keep doing what you're doing, listen to your guidance, and pay attention. You'll know."

~~~

In the animal totem a crow represents magic. Crows are incredibly smart and playful and know how to use tools and adapt to any situation. I heard the crow again.

"Things aren't always what they seem."

I was in awe. I was so close to a crow, and I knew of its magic and power, knew this wonderful moment was orchestrated just for me. I felt there was still more. I remained in the energy, frozen in time, as the message unfolded. That special nugget of wisdom came from near the trash can, a trash can most people would have passed by swiftly.

I studied the crow's body. The eyes, head, beak, amazing color, wings, and tail feathers. As I moved to looking at his legs, I noticed the bend of his left leg didn't match the right. It was disjointed or broken. He moved around the rim of the trash can by hopping on one leg and couldn't put his full weight on it.

Then the most amazing thing happened. I felt sorry for him, hopping around on the trash lid on one leg. I wondered if he'd be OK.

"Oh man buddy, is there anything I can do for you? That's gotta suck. Do you need any help? Is there something I can do for you?" I asked him.

With the strength, determination, and confidence of a warrior, he took flight high over the rooftops while sharing his last bit of wisdom.

"Things aren't always what they seem," he repeated, "and sometimes broken can be beautiful, just like you."

Chapter 16
Rebirth

Are you freakin' kidding me? What the hell am I supposed to do with THIS information? Maybe my energy was off. I'll try again another day.

I did. I tried again on a "good" day and received the exact same result. I felt equally defeated and validated.

Through the years I have experimented with all kinds of different ways to get to my core issues and heal them. I've read, attended therapy, had psychic readings, karma clearing, Akashic record readings, horse healings, family constellation work, spiritual retreats, sweat lodges, yoga, meditations, body work, energy work, and so many more. On this day I chose to listen to a timeline meditation.

It started with the usual disclaimer not to drive or operate heavy machinery while listening. The person's voice was velvety soft and soothing. They continued by encouraging me to lie down, dim the lights, and get comfortable. Soon I was being guided into deep breathing and other steps to relax my body and mind. Several minutes in the speaker told me to imagine myself standing in front of a giant timeline representing the different ages and stages of my life.

"Imagine yourself today," they said. "See yourself as you are now. Feel your body. Imagine as many details as you can."

After a pause the narrator asked me to start moving

backward through time, dialing back through the ages on the timeline.

"Go back further and further in time, slowly, carefully, checking in with yourself. Keep going back until the first time you felt less than."

So there I was, relaxed and comfortable, feeling supported by the stranger speaking, seeking answers. I scrolled back through the decades, through my fifties, forties, thirties, then going back further and further to my twenties, teens, and below. It was dark, warm, and smokey, and I was floating with something attached to my belly. I couldn't see anything, but I could feel and hear.

I heard a familiar female voice say, "I don't know what I'm doing. I don't even *want* kids."

I shook myself awake, somewhat in shock.

I did the meditation again several days later and received the same result. The message was clear: My mother didn't want me. Wow. How does one go about processing *that* information? How the hell do I heal from *that?* I felt so many things: shame, embarrassment, anger, frustration, sadness, isolation, unwanted, *and* validated. I was also faced with a fear of who to talk to about this. Who would understand and not minimize my experience? Who could possibly help me through this and not just blow it off? I couldn't think of a single person. Again, I was on my own. This was my secret, one of many.

The days and weeks passed. I had trouble concentrating, sleeping, and doing much of anything productive. Not being wanted by my own mother was beyond my comprehension. It explained a lot, though: the beatings, anger, behavior, and hatred toward herself. Every time she looked at me she was reminded of "her mistake."

As a child, I looked to her for love, protection, and guidance. I'd continue to seek it out despite often being shoved away. I'd still try desperately, hoping, yearning, wanting. I know now that she was emotionally repressed and completely unavailable. I also know *now* how her behavior toward me affected every single one of my relationships going forward.

I thought about all the good I've done to make the world a better place, my kindness to other people and animals despite having such a lousy start. *I deserve to be here*, I thought to myself. *I AM a good person. How can I reclaim this part of myself? What can I do to start over?*

~~~

My gym has a heated saltwater pool. Because of all the senior members, it's kept much warmer than most. I had the whole pool to myself one day. My swim this day felt different. Without other people's energy around me, I was able to truly immerse myself in the experience. I heard the whoosh of the water and got lost in the rhythm of my breathing. I felt the bubbles from my exhale tickle my face as they slid past my cheeks. It felt amazing and new.

I was still alone after finishing my laps when the thought occurred to me that I could rebirth myself—right here in the pool—right now! Hurriedly, I grabbed some pool noodles. It was important to complete this before others joined me in the pool. I tucked a couple under my armpits and across my back to hold up my upper body and a couple more behind my knees for the lower. Childlike, I giggled at my homemade floating recliner.

Once settled in I closed my eyes and imagined what it would be like in a loving womb. Being in the pool made that part easy. I floated effortlessly in the warm saltwater. My senses and imagination were fully engaged. My fingers and toes danced in the soothing water—safe, protected, loved. I imagined myself wiggling around, somersaulting weightlessly like an astronaut in space. Oh, how good this felt!

The people on the "outside" spoke and behaved differently during my rebirth. They were the same messed up people who greeted me the first time but I was able to imagine them anticipating my arrival with excitement instead of dread. Inside the womb I prepared myself to come out. I gleefully saw myself making my way down the birth canal like slipping down a giant water slide. "Whee."

Once out in the open I created the experience of being greeted the way a newborn *should* be greeted! There were smiles, exclamations of "she's adorable" and "oh, this is going to be so much fun" and "I'm so excited! I have a little sister!"

I floated in that pool for quite a while drinking it all in. It felt incredibly powerful to take charge and rebirth myself.

I've since shamelessly shared that experience with others in the hope they, too, may have the courage to recreate a part of themselves that someone else may have taken away. I've learned that if the truth doesn't set me free, my imagination will.

Chapter 17

Talking Smack

Being slapped snapped the dry-rotted rubber band that our relationship had become. Once fairly flexible and malleable, the band morphed into something completely unsustainable and out of balance—for me. Much of the crazy felt familiar because I had experienced similar situations in childhood, but it also didn't really "fit" me anymore. I was reborn. Healing. Growing. Learning. Speaking up for myself. Setting boundaries.

I remembered receiving so many mixed messages growing up, all the broken promises of alcoholic parents and a psycho sibling. These were normal and comforting like a favorite pair of soft, well-worn, flannel pajamas. But many also led to extreme disappointment and abandonment. As a kid, I held onto that "one good time" when someone actually kept their word or did something nice unexpectedly. This "normal" set me up for a lifetime of challenges in relationships and tolerating more crazy than I should have.

I found she was agreeable and supportive of things that afforded her an opportunity to look good or keep an eye on me but adamant about other stuff that threatened her fantasy of security. She liked to wield power over my choices. For example, she was by my side for events I presented at but was strongly opposed to me writing my first book. As the book began taking shape, I would occasionally share a story with her. I did so to be open about what I was working on, not because I needed her help or approval. When I received a draft cover design, she insisted I send it to her immediately.

When I agreed to show it to her the next time we were together but declined to "send it," she lost her shit and shouted, "You better not ask me for any more help with the book."

I had to hold back a chuckle. I reminded her that I was already working with a writers' group, an editor, a cover designer, and a photographer.

"I'll show it to you when I see you," I said. "It's just a draft." I felt she was incensed about not getting her way. I started to learn that people without boundaries don't like it when others try to set them. It threatens their feeling of being in control.

There were other times when she deliberately manipulated situations to get what she wanted. One weekend while staying at my house, she used the guise of having to return things to two different stores to spend the day bargain hunting. Not a fan of retail therapy and not wanting to spend the day doing it, I had a conversation with her before we left my house.

"I want to be clear that I'm not into shopping today. Please reassure me that you're *just* going to do your returns, then we're going to leave. If not, you go and I'll stay here."

She agreed. We went. She reneged and unapologetically justified her actions because things were on sale.

When we arrived back at my house, I replayed the day's events aloud, starting with the kitchen conversation before we left. I asked her if she remembered it. She said she did. Then we talked about what actually happened at both stores. I told her I *felt* manipulated. Furious, she turned my words around and asked me if I was calling her a manipulator. I said I wasn't calling her anything but rather telling her how it felt. The conversation went in circles. I started to learn about gaslighting.

Another time she tried to bait me into offering up my very small, tidy house to three of her family members who were planning a New York City adventure. One bought tickets to an event for another, and the third was their ride from Pennsylvania.

"Isn't it a nice thing she did by buying the tickets?" she would say.

I agreed but did *not* offer to be their lodging. The "nice thing" didn't involve me. I had flashbacks of a previous event when the trio rented a hotel room. It was a disgusting disaster. There were open food containers, wrappers, soda cans, makeup, costumes, glitter, and clothes everywhere. I stayed in my lane and refused to offer up my house. Eventually grudgingly and clearly annoyed when I didn't take the bait, she asked.

I replied honestly. "Listen, I saw what they did to that hotel room, and it makes me *very* uncomfortable."

She tilted her head, made the sad-eyed puppy dog face.

I *wanted* to be a good partner. I *knew* this was important to her.

"You stay at *their* house sometimes," she said.

Yeah, and you pay rent to stay there, and I clean up after myself. "OK" I said. "But here's the deal; it's only overnight. They come in, go to New York, do their thing, sleep here, and leave first thing in the morning. AND this conversation needs to happen with them ahead of time: no food, no costumes, no makeup, no mess, JUST overnight to sleep."

The conversation between us happened many, many weeks before said event. I said my piece, set a firm and reasonable boundary, and let it go.

A few weeks later my then girlfriend mentioned something about how excited everyone was about the trip. I asked if *she* had had the conversation about the stay with them.

"No, I didn't get the chance." *WTF, they live in the same*

house. Let it go. She knows but have a Plan B and be ready to hold firm.

As the weeks ticked by and the time was drawing near, I started losing sleep over it. *What were you thinking? Why did you agree to this?*

I was out her way about a week before said event.

"You know, they're excited about next weekend," she said as we had our morning coffee while side by side, each perusing social media.

"Next *weekend*? I only agreed to an overnight. By the way, did you have the conversation?"

I received what I was beginning to call "the look." "The look" is a creepy cross between a blank stare and a glare. I never did figure out the blank stare part but the glare represented anger for being called out and held accountable. *She* didn't like that.

The words "No, I didn't" hung in the air between us.

You're off the hook. She did this to herself. She didn't hold up her end of the bargain. She's had months. She's hoping you're just going to give in like you always have. What are you going to do?

I sent a link to a hotel near my house to the person sitting next to me with a note that said, "This is the best option for everyone at this point," then silently counted down in my head, "3...2...1"

"ARE YOU SERIOUS? YOU WANT THEM TO STAY IN A HOTEL? YOU'RE TAKING BACK THE INVITATION? I HAVE TO PAY FOR A HOTEL NOW? THAT'S GOING TO COST ME A FORTUNE!"

"YOU don't have to pay for anything. This is a teaching moment. When I was their age and if I didn't have the money to do or see or have something, I didn't do or see or have it. YOU agreed to have a conversation that you deliberately chose not to have and expected ME to just roll with it. That's not happening this time. I tried to be reasonable and compromise despite my discomfort about the whole situation, and YOU left me no choice but to enforce my boundary."

Softly and sweetly, nearly batting her eyes at me like a cartoon character, she tried re-baiting the hook. "But isn't it a nice thing they're doing?"

I replied firmly, "Yes, but their lodging truly doesn't involve me. I've already agreed to buy my own train ticket and be the tour guide for the day. That is the extent of what I'm willing to do."

Livid, she marched upstairs to deliver the news. Knowing her, I doubt she told the full story. I'm sure there were dramatic hand gestures and accompanying body language, disgusted facial expressions, and tsks and eye rolls involved in making *me* look really bad and *her* look really good. I had reached the point of not caring how she chose to behave *and* slept like a baby that night, knowing I did what felt right for *me*.

If these were isolated incidents spread really far apart, we might still be together—if she hadn't hit me, of course. But they weren't. They were selfish, self-serving, manipulative, narcissistic, and abusive acts of control that mirrored my childhood. I was learning gradually how to take my power back and that I *ALWAYS* have choices.

Chapter 18
I Chose Me

I chose.

I chose to stay even though there was a part of me that *knew* it didn't feel good or right but hadn't fully unraveled why. I *knew* she was rushing. She tried rushing my first overnight stay at her house, openly talking about *our* long-range plan, trying to make decisions for me or about *my* house or *my* things. I listened and learned and kept chugging along in the relationship, hoping it would get better. I communicated my needs and boundaries as best I could. I was developing new skills and practiced saying no.

Before she sold her house, there was much work to be done. I removed and replaced a number of rotted planks on the enormous deck that surrounded her built-in pool before repainting the entire thing with a brush on my hands and knees.

She helped some by handing me tools but would use any excuse to walk away. "Oh my sister's here. The dogs need to go out" or back in because they were so small and delicate. In fact, she carried a wooden club around her backyard to fight off the hawks she feared would pick off the dogs like the flying monkeys in *The Wizard of Oz*—hawks I never saw.

We spread mulch, moved a fire pit, cut branches, and rehabbed a vegetable garden. Inside, I patched and painted a fallen section of the living room ceiling, replaced a toilet in one of the bathrooms, and sanded and restained a portion of hardwood flooring where one of the delicates "had an accident." From the size and discoloration it looked like it was more than once. We worked in the attic, garage, and multiple outbuildings. I was out her way more frequently during that time, paying a cat sitter and putting my own projects on hold. I chose to. To keep her happy and keep the peace. I hadn't yet heard the term people pleaser. I thought I was being a good partner. *Surely, we would have time for fun again and my house projects when all this was done.*

As my birthday approached, she asked me what I wanted.

"Elton John tickets!" I answered excitedly.

She asked. I answered.

I got a lamp and clothes that were on sale. *WTF! A lamp? More clothes? Why did she even bother asking? This is NOT ok. THIS does NOT feel good.*

I stewed. I talked to trusted friends. "Am I being unreasonable? Asking for too much?"

My friends pretty much all responded the same way. "A lamp, Sherri? A fucking lamp? What were you supposed to do? Rub it for the tickets? Get rid of her."

Again, I chose to stay. *I'll talk to her about it.* And I did.

"Why did you ask me what I wanted and get me something else? Why no Elton tickets?"

"They were over $200," she said.

I agreed they could be pricey and pointed out that any ONE of the projects I completed at her house would have cost her at least that much if she hired someone. "You know, it's not bad enough that you *didn't* get the tickets but that you didn't tell me you had no plans to get them—essentially deciding *for me* that I didn't deserve them."

I received the blank glare look again.

I continued. "You dismissed my desire AND took my choice away, the choice to buy my own ticket. That is not OK. It is not OK to choose for me."

COVID showed up. Concerts and travel were canceled anyway. She was off the hook for now. Rubbing the lamp was no longer an option. I continued learning and welcomed the forced "two-week quarantine." *She* had different plans.

She thought *she* and her two delicate dogs were going to move in with me. The world had pretty much closed up, and she had tired of living in her sibling's basement. Real estate transactions and open houses as we knew them pre-COVID had halted her house hunting. I welcomed the quarantine and started a project that had been on *my* to-do list for twenty-seven years!

"You have to work anyway" I told her.

She reminded me that she could work from anywhere.

"That's not going to work for me. My project is the pantry in the middle of the house. Everything from inside the pantry is where you normally put all the stuff you and the dogs bring when you stay here. It doesn't feel good to be expected to be quiet in my own house while I'm working on a project that I've put off as long as I have because you have to work. There's the radio, the power tools, just no. Besides, it's only two weeks."

She *said* she didn't feel like she was welcome at my house. I think my newly laid boundaries started to make her feel like she was losing control of me. I never felt like I had control of me, and I was learning to do life differently. I was learning to communicate better, ask for what I needed, and put my needs first. It took practice, and I didn't always get it right.

The start of COVID was scary, and she lived with other people who were out and about in the world. I didn't. With the numbers rising I wasn't comfortable being around people I *knew* were around a lot of other people. She couldn't understand that.

Eventually, things started opening up again, and we resumed our "your place or mine" routine. She'd keep score of whose turn it was to travel despite my house being quieter, more comfortable, and having unfinished projects. And I started paying closer attention to my inner voices. One of the voices seemed to be telling me to work harder, and the other one began asking some tough questions. *Relationships are hard and take work. When was the last time she put YOU and YOUR needs first?*

During one particular weekend friends of mine agreed to help me with a basement waterproofing project. I told her it was best she and the dogs stayed home. She said she felt unwelcome and unqualified. The truth is: She and her dogs required my undivided attention, and I wanted to get the job done. It had also been on my list for some time. I noticed that trying to navigate her needs and insecurities was exhausting *and* not mine to manage.

During another weekend she had asked for "my help" installing a fence around her sister's garden. I also had things that needed doing that weekend so we had a conversation to negotiate.

"Before I come out I need to make sure you can help me with a couple of things," I said. "Otherwise, I'm going to stay put; these are important to me."

She agreed. What we didn't agree on was when I was to arrive. She was working until 11 p.m. Saturday night and wanted me "there" when she got home. I said I'd come in the morning.

I didn't like sleeping in the basement and hearing people walking above my head, and I couldn't very well tell them to be quiet in their own home either. I'm a light sleeper, *and* I know my comfort level. She thought I was being unreasonable. *If you love me you'll be here when I get home from work.* (Insert batting eyes.) I showed up Sunday morning with a trunk full of tools.

We could have easily installed adequate fencing by securing it to the inside of the existing railroad ties that framed the garden in a few hours, but she had to have it done *her* way—to exercise control over us minions. She wanted to dig holes and put the posts outside of the ties. I began with the post-hole digger I brought from home and hit rock. I moved a few inches and hit rock. I moved around the perimeter and hit rock.

Annoyed, she took the post-hole digger from me to "show me how to do it" and hit rock.

I took the digger from her and returned it to my trunk. "It's not designed for that. It's meant for grass and dirt, not rock." I said.

She didn't like being wrong—ever—and let out the sound an inflated balloon makes when you let it go, then marched away furious. You could almost see the wheels turning in her head and the smoke billowing out of her ears.

Her brother-in-law fetched a pry bar, and we began the painstaking process of removing rocks to get holes made. After a short time my girlfriend and her sister left us to go rent a one-man auger to speed up the post-hole digging. They left us in the hot summer sun and were gone over two hours. *Why did they both have to go? It sure feels like I'm doing more than just helping.*

The auger she abandoned us for because she had to have it? She learned the hard way that it wasn't designed to go through rock either. After the first day I was exhausted and had no energy left to work on my things.

She got me up extra early Monday to "get an early start." I thought it was so we'd have time to work on my things. Silly me. *Selfish people don't think that way.*

"I have an appointment to see a house at nine," she said.

"I'm coming, too."

"My sister's coming."

"I'm not going to be left behind working alone. This isn't MY project. I'm just supposed to be helping."

"My brother-in-law will help you."

"No, I'm coming with."

They left without me, and I worked with her brother-in-law—a man she couldn't stand. Then the cable company showed up and needed him. I continued working alone like a dumb ass. I stayed because I liked my girlfriend's sister and because I committed to the project. *Why? Why are you doing this? It's not even your fucking project. Just pack up your shit and leave. You're doing this for her sister. She's always been good to you. You're almost done, then you can leave.*

They returned, and I finished putting the lock on the homemade gate I made based on my girlfriend's specifications. Truly, it looked like a five-year-old's Popsicle stick art project. She had to have it *her way.* I thought it looked silly not finishing at the same height as the fence. What did I care? It wasn't my yard.

I said goodbye to my girlfriend's sister and brother-in-law, gathered up the last of my tools, and headed for the car. My girlfriend now tried to take credit for "getting me on the road early to get my stuff done." Astonished by her inability to see anything wrong with leaving me behind, not once but twice, even after repeating that I was coming to the open house with them, I spelled it out.

"It was NOT OK to be left behind to work by myself like that. You asked me to help. This was YOUR project, not mine. But I'm not blaming you. I'm the idiot who should have left YESTERDAY when you left the first time. THIS will not happen again. Not ever."

"Yes, but I'm getting you on the road early."

"No, I'm getting on the road early because I'M packing up my stuff and getting on the road and certainly NOT because of anything you've done. I hope you're happy, though. Your stuff is done, and I've learned another valuable lesson. I will be putting myself first more of the time." And I did just that.

The week before the fateful slap a friend invited me to camp on Assateague Island for a few days. "

YES! Friend time is just what my soul needs!" I didn't invite my girlfriend. I didn't ask for permission. I also didn't hide the fact that I was going or who I was going with.

"It better not be interfering with *OUR TIME!*" she demanded rather than asked.

"Nope, it's during the week. I'll be home in time for the horseback riding adventure."

I made my choice. I chose me.

What I didn't realize until it was far too late was that my self-loving choice pushed my then girlfriend completely over the edge. She was wound up tighter than any rubber band could ever stand. She snapped. I got slapped. And the relationship got zapped like a biting mosquito. And my friends all clapped!

Chapter 19
Good Grief

I felt grief. And was incredibly surprised by it. *What is this? She used you like a dish rag. She'd rinse you in fresh, clean, soapy water every now and again but she wrung you out to dry, used and abused. And then refused to see anything wrong with it. She deliberately disregarded clear and concise requests. Frequently. These were not misunderstandings. They were conscious choices to control you. For God's sake she HIT you…in front of your friends and then made it about her—about how embarrassed she was! She downplayed that she slapped a multiple abuse survivor! Why in the world are you sad about closing this door?*

I dug deep, and I felt things I hadn't been allowed to feel. Things that in my childhood home weren't safe to feel. They weren't safe because my caregivers didn't know to feel. I was the by-product of generations of emotionally unavailable people, and yet I grieved the loss. I was bewildered and kept digging for answers. *Why are you sad? You can't stay with someone who hurts you.*

I grieved the loss of her sister who would be forced to discontinue contact with me. I grieved the loss of her sister's *real* dogs—big dogs that could get on the furniture by themselves, do their business outside, hike for hours, carry their own gear, and walk through puddles and get dirty. I'd most certainly also miss the amazing meals and desserts she created whenever I was there.

I grieved the honeymoon phase of our relationship when she treated me like a partner and "allowed" me to have my own voice and choice, when there was still respect.

I grieved the perceived loss of four years of my life.

I reflected.

This woman mirrored much about how I *had* behaved in my life. Having no control over my childhood, for a time I unconsciously swung the pendulum in the complete opposite direction as an adult. She reflected back to me where I came from, where I was, and where I left.

I knew.

I *knew* I entered the relationship around the time I walked away from my entire living family. I *knew* I partially returned to dating as a distraction. I *knew* the early attention and travel felt good. I *knew* so many things but still couldn't grasp the grief.

I grew.

I *grew* into someone I could be proud of, someone who could set healthy boundaries, say no, and ask for what I need. I *grew* into someone who could communicate calmly despite being shouted at.

And then I got a clue.

The *clue* came in understanding how my hopelessly hopeful inner child bent the truth to survive childhood. The *clue* was my choosing continually to see some fantasy potential in others instead of courageously walking my own path. How I kept secrets to keep the peace in an effort to stay safe even though it really wasn't.

Belief relief.

My belief in grief was that it's bad or sad and therefore to be avoided at all costs. It's a feeling after all, and I was severely punished for those as a child. Internally, that belief never tracked with me but I never had a safe space to disagree. I finally have relief from that belief. In this instance I gained far more than I lost, and that I call *Good Grief.*

Chapter 20
Special Friend

She was the funniest, wittiest, most resilient, versatile, talented, generous, and gorgeous woman I had ever met. Equally comfortable in boy's Spiderman tighty-whitey underwear beneath her gardening outfit or softball uniform or sporting a slinky red dress with hooker heels, whatever she wore she looked amazing. This tall, slender redhead with a razor tongue and heart of gold was my friend and knew how to snap me out of a funk.

We met playing softball. If her looks and mannerisms didn't draw you in, her witty, spot-on one-liners certainly did. Catch her on an "off" day and they would spew out of her mouth ten times as fast. I remember my head spinning trying to keep up. Her sarcasm could turn the darkest of days into a comedy show. She loved so many things and people that it would be easier to say there were only a few things she didn't particularly care for—only a few. She loved plants and animals, sometimes more than people I'd guess, and cooking for others. Sometimes after softball game, she'd have the whole team back to her house where she had a full meal waiting for us. We used to refer to her as Martha Stewart on crack. The love and community she created was second to none. All were welcome.

She also had a passion for gardening. Her gardens were like something right out of *Better Homes & Gardens*. I asked for help to dress up a few spaces in my yard. She came over and looked at the areas, then we went back to her house to "shop." In no time flat, she brought the lonely corners of my yard to life with different grasses, greens, and flowers that would continue to multiply and fill in as they matured. In time I, too, would have plants to separate and share with others to plant in the bare spots in *their* yards. She taught me well.

Her life's resume was an interesting one. In addition to playing softball, gardening, catering, nurturing, teaching, and mothering, she also knew how to drive tractors and heavy equipment. She even did a stint as a bus driver for kids with special needs—yes, she loved each of those kids, too. There was a backhoe in the distance at one of our softball games. We were laughing and joking about something as our friend jumped up in the driver's seat. She would do just about anything for a laugh. Our laughter quickly turned to fear when the engine came to life and the tractor started moving. We were afraid she was going to get us all arrested that day! Then who would bail us out?

Memories of my friend were many, and she kept her word all but once. She vowed to beat her cancer and promised me another visit. The cancer took her life, but it could NOT take her free spirit.

~~~

A social media post from her life partner marking the seventh anniversary of her passing found its way into my feed. I publicly remarked on how she still "owed me a visit" and flat out said that I'd be watching for her magic that day. Within the hour she appeared.

I had been in my house for thirty-one years—thirty-one. Since I live within walking distance to many things, I frequently walk instead of drive. I headed out for a walk to the post office. In thirty-one years I have NEVER seen a school bus cruise down my street. NEVER EVER. With the most perfect of timing for my walk, the big yellow school bus rounded the corner and headed toward me. The bus driver, a woman, sat pretty and proud in her seat. As she passed I noticed she was smiling—just as my friend would have been. I smiled, knowing who was *really* at the wheel.

I rounded the corner and called her partner. While leaving a voicemail detailing my special visit, I spotted a shiny nickel next to a frozen pile of dog poop. I laughed. Her message—that it was really shitty that she had been taken so young. After hanging up I called to tell a friend the story of the bus and the nickel and found another coin, a penny. Still not convinced? When I arrived back home the mail had come. In that day's mail was a solicitation from the Special Olympics.

My friend was surely special and stayed true to her word.

Chapter 21

Three Crossing Guards
and a Stranger

The day started like any other, taking a walk to Dunkin' past the self-car wash vacuums in search of discarded stray coins. My little something told me to take the longer way home. I cut through the old neighborhood, past my former elementary school, chatted with one crossing guard about gardening and tomato cages, said hello to another on the next block, and reminisced with a third about a time when our small town only had one traffic light that was programmed to blink at 11 p.m. every night. It felt as though we both managed to freeze time and space momentarily to remember when life was slower and simpler, before "progress" forced us into constant motion. Together, almost as if connected, we turned our faces toward the sun and drank in her warmth. We welcomed the day's beauty before moving on to what came next for each of us. His morning shift was over, and I continued my walk.

~~~

She sat in a chair smoking a cigarette outside the small apartment she shared with her sister. I had not seen her there before when taking the "long" route home.

"I guess if you made it through the winter smoking, there's no chance you're going to stop now on a nice day like this," I joked with a smile. "Being a former smoker myself, I get it, I also used to smoke outside. I gave it up back in 1996 after I got chewed out by my oncologist during a follow-up visit after completing chemo."

She smiled nervously, not sure how to respond to a joke about a cancer treatment.

"It's ok, I'm good—I beat it."

She welcomed the update so I stopped to chat some more.

It was incredibly windy, and we watched Mother Earth inhale and then exhale a blue, runaway 10-foot x 10-foot popup tent that landed on its side in the intersection. An inhale brought the tent into a side street just out of view from the main road while an exhale forced the tent back onto the busier road. Sometimes the breath was slow and measured, other times it stuttered and sputtered. The tent moved in harmony with the "breath" and caused drivers to behave similarly. It was no surprise to me that this occurred just a few blocks away from that lone traffic light in town so long ago. Things like this aren't a coincidence. *There's more here,* I thought to myself. *It's important for me to keep chatting with this woman. I came this way for a reason.*

Heartbreak and hardship can't hide. They cannot be held and protected by folding your arms across your chest, crossing your legs tightly, and creating a smoke screen around yourself through chain-smoking. The wind blew me in your direction, and my heart followed. With my open heart I felt you struggling, even though you didn't say it. You felt safe to share a little bit about your situation. I heard you, and shared some of my history, which was much the same. I offered hope and encouragement. You silently offered a reminder of where I'd been and how far I've traveled.

We watched Mother Earth take another breath as her "lung" was tucked back into the side street. As we slowed down and reconnected to the moment we remembered, this, too, shall pass.

I talked about signs and how they're all around us. I pulled three pennies I had found at the car wash out of my back right pocket.

"See these," I said as I held them out in front of me. "These represent the three youngsters that I'm not allowed to see anymore because my family can't handle the truth about my sibling. I get signs like these every single day. Many times there are two coins together and one a ways away. The two together represent the twins and the third their sibling, born a few years later."

I pointed to a bird struggling against the wind on a nearby telephone wire. Every time she seemed balanced, the wind came and she teetered. She had to use her wings to keep from falling.

"See that" I said. "That's us; some days it's going to be easy to stand up and hang on and stretch our wings. Other days something outside of us is going to make it harder. Remember that bird: Remember that if she can do it, so can we. Look for the signs, ask for them, and get excited when you get them."

We said our goodbyes, and I left just as the town's public works men removed the tent from the windy street.

Almost instantly I was rewarded. By showing kindness to three crossing guards and a stranger, I received another undeniable sign that I am walking the walk I'm meant to be walking. On the edge of the sidewalk, folded in half with two corners folded down, was a dollar bill. Of course, I laughed. The wind was so strong it not only blew a tent up and out of its yard but back and forth across a busy street multiple times. Yet, this tiny little dollar bill managed to stay planted in my path.

I put the dollar in my back right pocket to keep the three pennies company while I smiled and walked the rest of the way home. *Hmmm,* I thought to myself as I approached my driveway. *Is this the next story for my book?* Immediately, penny number four was at my feet. "I guess so" was the response. *I wonder how I'm going to finish it.*

Once inside I grabbed my laptop and started writing. The story came easily since it was so beautiful and fresh. I reached into my back right pocket and took out the dollar.

"There's more there," I heard. "Unfold it. Look at the date." There it was—MY sign. The undeniable sign that my heart has come to know.

The year was 2017—the last time I was able to interact with those three kids.

"They think about you, too!" was the message and "just remember to breathe."

Chapter 22
Misery Loves Company

"I'm not in a hurry to do that again," I said.

"Me neither," my new friend repeated.

My new confidant and I became fast friends as we shared the horrors, pains, and shortcomings of our exes. We shared story after story of how they didn't hear us or mistreated us and fell short of what we wanted or expected from them. Her ex was a guy, mine was not. In my mind she was "safe" for me to pal around with because she wasn't into women. There were ZERO expectations. The built-in bonus was she had split custody of two kids and a dog I was fond of. At the time they were a great distraction that spelled the trifecta of fun! I hadn't yet learned that distractions aren't always a good thing.

When the kids were around, activities focused on them. I'd bring their favorite doughnuts for after-soccer matches or root beer and ice cream for floats as an after-dinner treat. Every month I'd get three craft projects at the hardware store that we would work on together as an activity. In fact, they got so comfortable with me that they started calling me aunt, and that felt nice.

If the kids were with their dad, we either hung out together complaining about others or we would go out to dinner with some of the people that we talked about. It was slightly weird but seemed to work. We started to learn about each other's likes and dislikes and what didn't work in our previous relationships. Some of our stories were similar and some not. I listened carefully and shared openly.

She liked shopping. I did not. She liked buying things she thought others needed and would show up unannounced regularly and say, "Here, I got this for you." Then she would leave before you could say "NO!" I had also been the recipient of her personal discards—flowery bathing suits I wouldn't be caught dead in, a hooded Mexican poncho, a necklace she tired of, and a foot massage machine that I had no place to store or use—just to name a few. Each of these was a "drop and run" with the farewell of "if you don't like it, just donate or re-gift it." *Why don't YOU just donate or re-gift it? I have enough of my own stuff to take care of.*

On the rare occasion when *she* drove somewhere, sometimes I felt I was being held captive. "I know you don't like shopping but," she'd say, and we'd find ourselves at Ross, T.J. Maxx, or some other horrific place I really didn't want to be at.

It's better than being home alone, I suppose.

Early on she was very polite and would *ask* for my help with things or create an exchange for handy work by making or buying dinner. As she got more comfortable, she stopped asking and started demanding and expecting. Take the garbage out, re-hang the banister, walk the dog, pick up dinner, talk to the boys about their behavior. It all happened so gradually that I didn't really take notice until it was completely out of control and I found myself feeling used. *Again.*

I can still remember the conversation that sounded the alarms in my head. "Your car is always so clean," she said.

"Yeah, thanks. That's because I don't let anybody eat or drink in it."

"I'm going to pay you $100 to detail mine so I know it'll be done right."

Astonished, I said nothing. Sometime later she brought it

up again. Once again I froze and said nothing. I couldn't speak. The moment resembled a familiar recurring childhood nightmare, one in which I was in imminent danger and tried to scream for help but nothing came out.

Angry words formed in my head and stayed there. *I'm not cleaning your fucking car. I didn't make the mess, I'm not cleaning it up either.*

What the hell? How did I get here? Again? Why can't I speak up for myself?

I stewed over the encounter and can still feel myself getting pissed over the demand *and* my inability to push back. I never did clean her car, but the whole experience made me wonder why I behaved (or didn't behave) like an adult. That event and the "friendship" that eventually ran its course definitely left a mark on me. It had me questioning what vibe I was giving off and why I struggled to say NO! In time the source of this behavior would unravel.

Chapter 23
Progress

June 2022. I saw you today. It was the first time in over four years. You, the first and worst of my abusers. I was walking to the store, about to approach the crosswalk. Thanks to you and the undeserved torture and abuse you repeatedly thrust upon me, I have heightened sensitivities. I am always hyper aware of my surroundings, always scanning, feeling, listening, watching. Always. Thanks to your evil actions toward me, the safety guidance system inside me rarely takes a break. It has to. I have to keep myself safe.

I saw a black car headed south on Main as I walked the sidewalk north. I recognized the make and model, same as yours. The sun was shining, and it was incredibly hot and humid considering we were barely a week into the official start of summer.

I'd seen this kind and color of car many times since becoming the family outlaw—many times. Each time my body reacted. Each time my body *automatically* went into fight or flight mode. Each time, every…single...cell...reacted as if it were in imminent danger, about to be snuffed out. I would immediately feel the powerful surge of adrenaline course through my body in an effort to keep me safe. Each time I saw a black car the same model as yours panic washed over me and stayed until I saw the driver. Every. Single. Time. For years. Thankfully, it was never you until today.

As the car drew closer, I lowered my baseball cap-covered head as I approached the crosswalk. I lifted my eyes under the cap's brim just enough to see the driver and any occupants without being obvious about it. It was you *and your little dog, too.* Ok, so it wasn't really your little dog. I digressed into the witch from *The Wizard of Oz's* voice. It was actually your youngest adult kid, almost forty-two years of age at the time, in the passenger seat, head down, cell phone in hand.

I *know* you saw me, too. I *saw* and felt your reaction: a split-second tensing of muscles as you gripped the steering wheel tighter in a panic. I also *know* you didn't say a word to your passenger about seeing me. Those worms are all still better left in the can—for you.

I immediately phoned my new girlfriend. She was amazing with these kinds of things and seemed to know how to talk and walk me through such moments. She asked me how I was and what I was feeling.

"I feel like a giant monkey is on my back, trying to suffocate me." I could feel this big, black, hairy blob squeezing me from behind, arms wrapped around my chest. I felt its warm, steamy exhale on the back of my neck, its head pressed against mine.

It wasn't a "real" monkey, the kind of monkey I can communicate with, and I wasn't exactly in work mode either. I was just walking to the store, minding my own business—much like my childhood. I'd be in the backyard playing, by myself or with my dog Snooper, when all of a sudden I'd get dragged into the house by my ponytail. Because YOU were bored. Because YOU told Mommy I did something I didn't, and she believed you.

Consciously, I drew big, deep breaths as I continued walking and talking and worked to calm myself. The most incredible thing happened: The monkey got smaller. In only a few minutes, the monkey representing the incredible power and control you had over me for so long was shrinking, just like the witch in *The Wizard of Oz*. Your black car, representing the witch's hat, faded away in the distance as my own power returned. I could feel my heart rate start to return to normal, much faster than I ever would have expected. The tightness in my chest vanished, and so did the monkey!

My girlfriend asked me what I was thinking.

I responded with half a chuckle and said, "Here come the crazy thoughts."

"Crazy thoughts? Like?" she returned.

"Well, I have this vision of me—"

"Yeah?"

"Jumping on the hood of her car, like a flying monkey, pounding on the windshield calling *her* names and being menacing. I *know* it's my wounded inner child, the one who didn't have a voice or a choice back then. I can *see* her...me...the little me...from so long ago...fantasizing about retaliating...returning the fear."

In those brief moments I *saw* my younger inner self, *felt* her, in ways I hadn't been able to up until now. I continued breathing deeply, talking it through with my girlfriend, feeling loved, supported, and appreciated as an adult all while loving, supporting, and *seeing* my wounded inner child. *Being* a witness to my own inner child healing while *having* a witness was incredibly validating, powerful, and loving.

We talked more about the "divine timing" of only seeing them rather than actually running into them in the store I was headed to. We talked about how *that* might feel and what it might look like going forward. I realized how the tables have turned and how my very real fear has transformed into fearlessness. I no longer fear my sibling, and I suspect they fear *me* now. Not because of what I might *do*, but because of what I might say—or in my case what I might write.

The injured, repressed parts of me are surfacing to be healed. I am finally finished living in fear of my sibling, finally free of feeling less than the full expression of who I really am and what I deserve in this lifetime.

And that is progress.

Chapter 24

Close Call

"I'm ok, I'm ok, I'm ok....I'm safe...I'm safe...
SHIT! NOW WHAT?"

Danny was the sweep guide, the last boat on our rafting trip, and he couldn't paddle in to get me. He half-shrugged his shoulders in a gesture of "sorry" as he floated down river to join the rest of the trip. I found myself on top of a rock in a class II rapid known by two equally ominous names, Deaton's Demise and Killer Falls. Grateful doesn't begin to explain how I initially felt being in that predicament, safe for the moment.

It was a sunny Sunday on a dam release weekend. I got to the rafting center and organized my gear before guests started to arrive. Hydrate, coffee, lunch, shoes, helmet, paddle, personal flotation device (PFD), dry bag. Check. The vessel I would paddle for the trip—an inflatable kayak or IK as we river guides called them—would already be at the river's edge, the place we called the "put in." Pee, fill water guns, secure keys, double check pockets. Check. I was all ready for the 10:30 a.m. check-in. People began trickling in. And trickle they did.

I mixed and mingled as I got to know those who showed up on time. There were two single women and a family of three that I introduced to each other so they could all paddle together in one raft. We also had a group of eight who were given the trip as a holiday gift from their "afraid of the water" mom. Two of them admitted they inherited her fear.

"I understand the fear," I said.

They looked at me in disbelief. Their eyes seemed to say, "Oh great, we get stuck with the river guide that's afraid of the water."

"It's true," I said. "This is my fifth season as a guide. I started a long time ago, sitting where you are, as a guest. I'd come every year with my softball team or other friends. Not one of them knew I couldn't swim, not one of them knew how terrified I was of falling out of the raft. Every year I deliberately and carefully chose who would be in my raft so I could feel safe.

"True story," I told them. "My sibling tried to drown me as a youngster, not just once but many times. I had an unhealthy fear of the water for much of my life. Several years ago I walked away from that family and decided to start actively working through the water fear, and I showed up here for guide training. I was still scared but knew from all the trips I'd taken with this outfitter that I was in good hands."

The guests listened intently.

In those moments I realized how far I'd come. And how comfortable I was sharing my fear so openly. It felt good. The shame was gone, too.

"Will you stay close to us, Sherri?" they asked.

"Absolutely!" And I meant it.

~~~

"Something's not right. There should be more people here by now, I thought to myself. The center was missing the familiar buzz of activity that usually occurs at safety briefing time. A large group was running extremely late. Their tardiness began to unravel our well-oiled machine. A language barrier further complicated matters and put everyone into high gear—the gear that's normally reserved for the actual paddling trip, once everyone's on the water.

~~~

Our center's people moving skills usually resembles that of a calm fire drill: orderly, single file, one route. Everyone follows the same procedure. Waiver, life jacket, safety briefing, buckets, paddle, bus pass, board the bus, get on the water. A bird's-eye view would show a neat and orderly line with an occasional outlier maybe sprinting off to the rest room or running something back to their car. On this day I'm fairly certain the scene from above looked like someone had dropped a bucket of drunken marbles. There were people scattering in every direction, sometimes changing direction after a few steps. It was not the norm; the latecomers' erratic movements affected the energy of the entire trip. Since I hadn't slept well the night before, it began to feel as if I was trying to push a noodle uphill with my nose. "You'll feel better once you're finally on the water," I told myself.

The late group was put on the second bus while the early and on time folks were on the first bus with me.

"WOOHOO! We are *finally* on our way!" I said to the bus full of guests who were understandably just about out of patience. "Thank you, thank you, thank you all SOOOO much for your patience this morning. It was a whole lot of waiting around, way more than usual, and I thank you!"

I moved myself into my "cheery and engaging river guide" persona and continued to connect with this half of the group.

"Raise your hands if this is your first time."

Several hands went up.

"This is a school bus. Please remain seated and keep your hands and paddles inside."

After a few chuckles I asked if anyone was celebrating something special and two hands shot up. The whole bus sang Happy Birthday to both guests, one right after the other.

"Sit tight and enjoy the ride. We'll be at the put-in in about ten minutes. I'll tell you what comes next when we get closer and, again, thank you so much for your patience."

~~~

We are off to a rough start I thought to myself. It's going to be a lonnnng day if I can't turn it around. Or at least my own thoughts and attitude.

~~~

The end of August is a rough time of the year for me, and despite my best attempts to pre-plan for it by keeping myself busy, dark thoughts slither in. I try dressing them up by reframing them. I try telling myself I'm ok and that I'll be ok, that I've been here before and it will pass. It may pass like a kidney stone, but it will pass. I try desperately to be my own cheerleader, reminding myself how far I've come and not to be so hard on myself. *Grief takes time. You're where you're supposed to be...on the water. Water represents emotion. Let the river take your tears. Just breathe. Let Mother Nature and the river hug and nurture you. Enjoy the day with eighty-five strangers and your river family. Just let them love you today.*

~~~

I sat down and ate my pre-trip sandwich, ham and cheese with spicy mustard on a keto sandwich thin. River guides burn a lot of calories on trips. I do best when I'm well-fed and hydrated before I even start. Nobody likes a hangry river guide including me!

~~~

"Alllll right, everybody! We are just about to the 'put-in,' and here's what's gonna happen. The guides are going to get off first, and you all are going to storm the beach. I want you to get in the rafts closest to the water. We are going to get you guys launched ahead of the other group. Watch your step and LET'S GO!"

I jumped off the bus with my gear and held out my paddle like a traffic cop to keep my group up in front. *THIS is the way people on a mission move.* The front of the trip worked together and were orderly. The back of the trip, well, not so much. *At least they're consistent.*

Raft after raft was launched. Each made its way down river to the gathering point above the first and worst rapid of the day. This is the guide's "first look" at who has paddled before, who paid attention to instructions, and who may be in over their head. I remember thinking, *Rut roh, gonna be a lonnnnng day.*

As the trip leader was explaining what was going to happen next, I weaved in and around the rafts. I checked in on the two singles I had paired up with the family of three. I checked in on the group of eight, now split into two rafts with four men in one and four women in the other.

"You'll stay close, Sherri, right?" the women asked.

"Of course," I responded.

I paddled around making corrections, offering suggestions.

"Try turning your hand this way. It may be better if you put your feet over here. Please tuck the phone inside your life jacket when you're not using it." I'm all about safety and prevention.

We had five guides on this trip: a point, three roams, and a sweep. The point guide is the trip's mother duck. They know where the obstacles are and the best way down river; they also know where our lunch stop is! Sweep is the last person of the trip, your last hope to get "unstuck" if that happens. Roam guides do just that: We roam around the trip. Our job is to position ourselves on or near hazards that we want guests to avoid, and to assist them before the sweep guide gets to them if they get stuck or run into trouble. The trip leader was one of the roam guides, as was I.

Whelp, here we go, I thought to myself as we started paddling toward Deaton's. Most of the rafts were going exactly where they were supposed to be going, right down the middle. All but one.

"You'll stay close Sherri, right?" I heard in my head as I saw the group of four women drift toward river right. They were doing the best they could to change course, but the current was much faster than their correction strokes. Guests are told in the safety briefing, "Your raft goes where you look." The women were staring down at a rock approaching quickly, and I was watching it unfold from behind. I heard it again, "You'll stay close Sherri, right?"

It happened swiftly. Their raft went up and halfway over the rock with me close behind. As promised. I know NOT to approach a stuck raft from above. I know better. The current above a rock is wicked. My inflatable kayak and I went in hot. Before I could blink, my kayak was upside down, under their raft. Fortunately for me, I was not still IN the kayak. My left hand clung to my paddle while bracing it against the tilted raft.

"You ok, Sherri?" I heard from over the edge of the raft. "What can we do to help you?"

"Take my paddle," I said.

At some point I looked down to see that the raging current had partially unzipped my PFD; I quickly zipped it back up. My hands were braced against the stuck raft as my feet did their best to stay atop the wobbly IK. The raft's sides were rigid and firm, while the inflatable kayak's were not. Underneath me the IK buckled when I tried using it as a step to climb up into the raft. I lost my footing briefly and swallowed some of the Lehigh River. I gave up standing on my IK and clung to the safety rope around the raft. I had to get myself into a safer position before the Lehigh decided to retaliate and swallow me.

"You ok, Sherri? The other guide is here, and he wants us to move to the other side of the raft," one of my water-fearing ladies asked.

"Yeah, I'm good. Go ahead. Do what he says." I responded.

By now I was using the raft's safety rope to pull myself to a better spot on the rock, away from the wickedest part of the upstream current. The threat of being sucked underneath a raft had gone. The threat was replaced by "I'm ok, I'm ok, I'm ok. I'm safe, I'm safe. Then once Danny passed, "SHIT! NOW WHAT?"

In those moments time stood still. Danny drifted down and around the bend to join the rest of our guests. The trip lead, a seasoned veteran guide, waited for me downstream at the bend with my paddle-less kayak. As calmly as I could, I weighed my options while realizing I was calmer than I would have been a few years ago if I were in this predicament. *You're ok, we're ok*, I heard inside my head.

What happened inside my head next went something like this. *Slide in on the upstream side of the rock? Nope. Off to the right? Nope. What about the downstream side? Too far of a drop, foot entrapment, foot entrapment! What about the—Look upstream! Look upstream!*

To my surprise a couple and child were coming down with a guide. Their guide was in a kayak, but they were in a river catamaran. It is an extremely stable watercraft that looks like a pontoon boat and catamaran had made a baby and then shrunk it. Oars instead of paddles are used to propel it. They paddled in close enough for me to ask if they were able to get me. The couple pulled into the eddy behind the rock, and I leapt on board to the canvass area between the two paddlers.

"I can't thank you two enough," I said.

They paddled us downstream to my waiting trip leader and kayak. I still had to get back into my kayak and finish the trip. Another three-plus hours! The water here was extremely deep, and I was nearly out of adrenaline. After a few attempts I landed back in my kayak, but it didn't feel the same. It didn't feel as safe. My trip leader handed me his paddle.

"Don't lose this," he said. "I have some hand paddles that I can use until we get your paddle back."

We met back up with the trip, and I retrieved my paddle from the women.

"You ok Sherri?" they asked.

"Yeah, I lost one of my water guns and, unfortunately, my Chap Stick so I won't be able to freshen my makeup at the lunch stop. This is just going to have to do," I said as I waved my hand in front of my face.

"Damn, that was a close call," I said to myself as we continued downstream while I forced myself to stifle the intense shakes that accompanied the realization of what *could* have happened. Later that day and for several days my brain spliced together a loop of other memories that also caused terrible internal shakes. And my body reacted accordingly. Having unraveled much of the source of such deeply embedded terror, I now have better tools to address and self-soothe the frightened little girl inside of me.

It's been less than a week as I write this. The emotions around the event, the choices I made, the lessons, the "what ifs" and possible consequences of choosing differently continue to ebb and flow. I've stopped gasping in horror when I replay the scene in my mind. I do not regret for a minute "staying close" to offer comfort to our guests that were fearful.

I am extremely grateful to my river family and the couple who rescued me. I know when things seem hopeless, help is literally just around the bend, and all I have to do is ask.

Like life, the river is an amazing teacher. I can play it safe. I can follow the crowd downstream, avoiding obstacles, or I can take a different route. Like the warrior that I am, I have consciously chosen to face the obstacles head-on and stretch my limits. We will both make it down the river and will both have a story to tell. My story is about overcoming obstacles and fear.

What direction will yours take?

Chapter 25
Granddad Grief

The pain was the most intense I had ever felt in my life. It swallowed me with the fierceness of a raging river. I was submerged in a constricting pool of grief struggling for my next breath...my next thought...my next anything. I had to sit in it... forced to feel it. The sheer weight of that pain made it hard to breathe, hard to move, and, in those moments, virtually impossible to believe that I would ever move past it.

When the pain was too much to bear, I would leave my body. With intention, I would command my soul to leave my body and take a break. "Help me, .please help me." I could hear this otherworldly being say: "What is this? What do I need to know? To learn? To heal?"

Coming back into my body, "Please," I would beg. "Please make this feeling go away. Help me. Please take it. I surrender. Show me. Teach me."

~~~

I have done enough meditation, yoga, and energy work to be able to "come and go" from my body at will. It is a learned skill that has helped me grow, heal trauma, and view events from different perspectives for myself and others. When I remember to use it, it helps me move through difficult emotions with more grace and ease.

~~~

I sat in the garage in my favorite anti-gravity chair shocked and dumbstruck of being "let go" via written words—this was the second event in seven days done this way. The first, being booted from a team, was almost immediately seen as a blessing in disguise and sent me to a better place within days. But this one threw me for a loop. I was crushed.

My ball cap was pulled low as I held my head in my hands, sobbing. Through clouded eyes filled with tears, I watched the stream of snot ooze from my nose as it joined my salty tears in a growing puddle on the cement floor. I cried. I sobbed. I gasped for my next breath. My body was shuddering with the sudden flood of so much emotion at once. I was scared. I was so scared it would never, ever stop. In those moments I could not gain access to all the wonderful tools I have amassed along my personal healing journey. I was stuck in a pool of unbearable grief. At that moment I felt like a dog's dingleberry cut loose with a butt drag. Admittedly, I may be a "shit" sometimes, but not like that! I finally managed to summon the strength to phone a friend and to hang on like a dingleberry until they arrived.

We talked, I cried, they held space and listened. I'd settle down, blow my nose, and breathe for a few minutes before the feelings would well up and wash over me again. They felt so big and heavy and constricting. "Why? Why am I here again? What did I do wrong? This hurts SOOOO much, this hurts more than I ever remember. This hurts more than when my mom died or anybody or any pet or anything else I can remember. WHY!?" I searched my friend's face for answers.

Calmly, she replied "You're open now, you're really open. All the healing work you've done on yourself has led you here: to *really* feel and work through your emotions."

"It feels so big, it hurts so much. Too much. Does it ever end?" I asked.

After a long pause my friend answered. "It never really goes away; it lessens over time, and you're able to manage it better. I'm sorry, sweetie."

We sat quietly for a while as I digested all that had erupted in such a short period of time. My friend was the first to speak.

"Listen, I'm getting hungry. Now either you're going to cook me some eggs or I'm going to take you out for breakfast."

"I'm not cooking."

"OK, you choose the diner then."

"Yep, let me close up the garage, and we can go."

~~~

The place was packed with the Sunday morning church crowd. I summoned my angels and guides to give us a close parking spot and a short wait to be seated. Both were granted. We got a booth in the back, close to the bathrooms. Two glasses of water were brought to the table instantly, and our waitress appeared shortly thereafter.

"Tomato juice with lemon," I said.

"I'll have the orange juice, large," replied my friend.

"Uh, I think we're ready to order, too, if you want to get it all out of the way at once."

"Sure," our waitress obliged.

My friend ordered the Huevos Rancheros with a long story that amounted to "NO CILANTRO!" I ordered two eggs, basted, with corned beef hash and rye toast. My friend and I idly chatted as we waited for our breakfast. I couldn't help but wonder how it was going to sit since this was my first attempt at food since puking my morning coffee three times after receiving the "let go" message. Much to my surprise, I wasn't repulsed at the sight of my dish and ate most of it. And it stayed down.

After breakfast we were headed back to my house when another wave of grief surfaced and spewed out. "This isn't just about today's grief," I heard the dialogue in my head say. "Huh? What?" another voice replied. "This isn't just about today." I heard again. "What then? Where is this coming from?" I thought about it and why this hurt so much, so much more than I ever remember.

I half-left my body and dreamily recalled a conversation from six years ago with my friend who was currently driving me. That previous conversation came at the heels of being deeply triggered at a family picnic, which resulted in the realization that I was abused by my one and only sibling. In that historic conversation, my friend asked, "Have you ever felt like this before? Tell me about that."

I came back to the present moment and asked myself that first question, "Have I ever felt like this before?" then waited for an answer. As we rode down Main Street toward my house, it came to me: *old, unprocessed grief.*

"Can we take a detour?" I asked my friend.

"Sure, sweetie. Where?"

"The cemetery. I need to go to the cemetery," I said, sobbing yet again.

"OK, tell me how to get there."

~~~

We arrived at the cemetery as my tear banks filled to overflowing again and my aching heart burst open.

The lump in my throat, burning with the angst and fury of a ten-year-old's unspoken words to her dead granddad. Words that needed to be said, feelings that needed to be felt and completely validated and understood. Those feelings, huge feelings for a ten-year-old, were forcibly shoved down by the emotionally unavailable people who surrounded me back then. They were checked out themselves.

I fell to my knees by Gramps' headstone. I lovingly and painfully reached out to touch his name, to stroke the letters etched in the marble. My fingers traced some of them like a child feeling something new for the first time: the smoothness of the marble, the edge where the marble dipped in to form each letter, the roughness of the cavern that created each groove. I touched. I felt. I cried. I spoke—not eloquently like an adult but like a child who had just lost the only person in the world she felt truly loved her.

~~~

I left my body and imagined kneeling behind my ten-year-old self. My strong, steady, and loving hands were on her shoulders as my friend's hands were on mine. "What do you need to tell him? What do you want him to know?" I whispered inside my head.

"I love you, Gramps, and I miss you terribly. I miss playing cards and drinking root beer and burping and farting at the kitchen table with you. I miss your toothless grin, bright eyes, and loving heart. You showed me so much love, made me feel important, seen, and wanted. I miss riding your tractor around the yard and playing with your pet skunk. I even miss putting the paper and tobacco in your cigarette rolling machine! I know you've been around. I feel you with me sometimes. I *know* it's been you that's protected me. I just know it!"

My ten-year-old self, supported by my adult self, put it all out there, everything we wanted to say, everything we *needed* to say for so long. We felt it, too. We felt all of it. In that moment we felt all the grief piled on from forty-seven years of different life experiences resulting in some form of loss.

Without waiting for my dear friend to ask me what losing my grandfather was like, I began to tell the story.

"My parents fought a lot. I remember a lot of yelling and arguing. I don't remember what it was about, I just remember being woken by shouting—often. They decided to divorce. Around the same time my Gramps was in the hospital and not doing well. I remember vividly the conversation that occurred before visiting him in the Intensive Care Unit for what would be the last time. This was the one and only time I can remember when time was being taken to explain something to me, to prepare me. My mother and her then boyfriend, who eventually molested me, told me this.

"'Gramps is sick in the Intensive Care Unit at the hospital. We want to take you to see him but need you to know he's hooked up to all kinds of machines and it might be scary. He won't be able to talk to you because he has a tube in his mouth, helping him to breathe. But he *will* be able to hear you so you can talk to him and let him know you're there. We need you to be brave for Gramps. OK?'

"I can remember my ten-year-old self nodding and thinking, 'I have to be brave for Gramps.'

"We tiptoed into his room. I'm not sure why because the sound of all the machines would have masked the sound of any footsteps we might have made. I approached his bedside as I looked around at all the equipment that was going to make Gramps better. Some of it beeped, some of it whooshed. There were clear bags of medicine hanging from poles. The bags had tangled tubes that came out the bottom like spaghetti noodles. The clear 'noodles' traveled from the bottom of the bags down along the side of Gramps' bedsheets and into his arm—held in place with white tape. There were wires, too. Wires that came from a beeping machine in the corner. It resembled a small television set with a bunch of lines and numbers in different colors on it. The wires extended from the machine down along the other side of Gramps' bed and the ends were taped to his bare chest. 'Be brave for Gramps,' I heard inside my head. And I was.

"Someone, likely my mother's boyfriend, told me it was ok and encouraged me to move closer, to touch him, to talk to him.

"'Let him know you're here,' they said.

"I remember the scene. I remember being there. I remember

everything about the room and the sounds and the smells. I don't remember the actual moment of touching Gramps for what would be the last time. I don't remember what I said but I know I spoke to 'let him know I was here and that I loved him and wanted him to get better.' I don't know if it was my touch or my voice or both but Gramps responded immediately to my presence. The machines went bonkers, and people started rushing into the room.

"'Suction, suction,' I heard. I watched someone grab what looked to me like a magic wand, and they stuck it down Gramps' throat tube and sucked out a thick liquid that resembled snot. It sounded like when the dental hygienist sucks the spit out of your mouth during a cleaning.

"'He knows you're here,' someone said as happily as they could manage. 'He can't talk but this is his way of letting you know he knows.'"

Tearfully, I told my friend that was the last time I saw my Gramps.

"Wow," my friend said. "Good thing they took the time to have that very important conversation with you, to prepare you."

"Yep," I replied. "I was ten and didn't understand what was really happening, why I was *really* there. I know now that that moment prepared me for a lifetime of being comfortable in the hospital setting, to be of service to others, to be brave. It was definitely a defining moment."

"What happened next?" my friend asked.

"Well, there was another conversation to prepare me for what may happen next," I continued. "There were two things going on sort of simultaneously: Gramps' dying and my parents' court date for divorce. So I was told that if my sibling picked me up from school, it was because of one of those events. I can still picture my dad's navy blue Pontiac Bonneville parked on the curve of the parking lot near the elementary school gym with my sibling in the driver's seat. I opened the passenger door and slid in.

"'Well, which is it?' I asked. 'Did Grampa die or are Mommy and Daddy divorced?'

"The response was that Grampa died. We rode in silence.

"The wake and funeral were a shit show. There were no explanations, no talk of heaven or what would happen to Gramps. I remember feeling my grandmother's anger for having to pay for her ex-husband's funeral. Because he was 'a loser,' she said. Drank and gambled his money away. I remember seeing my mother cry and smelling cigarettes and stale alcohol on her breath. I remember seeing Gramps sleeping in a box in front of the room, peaceful and free from tubes, wires, and machines. I remember the amazing smell of all the flowers around the box he slept in. I wondered when he was going to wake up. I searched the hearts and faces of those in the room for answers. None came.

"Finally, I asked, 'What's going on? What does this mean?'

"My seventeen-year-old sibling stormed by and shouted in my face, 'It means he's dead, gone, you're never going to see him again. They're going to close the box, put it in the ground, and the worms are gonna eat him.' I don't remember what followed that conversation. I do remember the next day. The graveside.

"The box that carried Gramps was set in a steel contraption with wide green straps that held the box in place on top of a huge hole in the ground. A green carpet of fake grass surrounded the hole, and several chairs were placed on one side. People were sad and crying. The air was thick. It was hard to breathe, almost as if the box was already in the ground and covered with dirt. Suffocating."

"That's a lot," my friend said. "That's a lot for a ten-year-old to manage."

"Yes, it is," I agreed.

"Still kneeling in the grass by the headstone, I came back

into the present moment, now somewhat settled and back in my body. I asked, 'Gramps, you there? Did you hear me?' I didn't have to wait long before I smelled fresh flowers, like you'd smell in a funeral home. I looked down at the half-dead rose bush that separated Gramps and Grandmom's names on the stone. I paused, wondering if the amazing aroma could possibly be coming from the pathetic planting before me. I bent down to take a whiff from a few of the wilting red roses. I had my answer. Gramps was there. 'Thank you, Gramps,' I whispered. 'I love you, too.'"

What next? Stand up, stand up and face the sun.

I rose and took a quarter turn left to face the sun. My body felt different. I didn't rise with the defeated posture of a traumatized and abused kid who just got pushed off the plate like some unwanted peas. I rose like the spiritual warrior that I've become. My shoulders were not rounded to protect my aching heart from a breakup message delivered in such a cowardly fashion by someone who claimed to love me. On the contrary, my shoulders were back, and my heart was wide open. It was open to receive the love and light from the sun. I willed my true mother of sustenance, Mother Nature, to fill my heart and soul back up with all she had. The warmth of her rays began burning off the layers of grief and extreme sadness. My ten-year-old self began the healing process and delighted in watching the clouds change shapes—finally feeling seen, heard, and validated.

"There's so much information here for me," I said to my friend as I slowly and deliberately turned around to receive it with outstretched arms. I heard the loud jeers of a blue jay to my left and the whistles of a cardinal to my right. Both birds called back and forth several times until I told them I received their messages. They reminded me to take flight and to carry their spiritual medicine with me. What the birds shared made me dizzy. I kicked off my shoes and walked barefoot in the grass. Then I grabbed a tree and forced myself to come back into my human body. The pain and grief felt smaller now, more manageable. But I wasn't done. I took a last look around, and there it was: the tree that represented my life.

The tree leaned to the right. Its base was being choked by vines. The vines appeared to belong because they were green and healthy; in reality, they were holding on tightly for a free ride "up" and to feed themselves. Above the vines was exposed bark that led up to a number of branches. This section's limbs were dead and broken off at various lengths. They represented a variety of people, experiences, and beliefs that have come and gone from my life. Some were short and stubby while others were long and thin. Each served its purpose but was eventually lopped off. Next was an area with sparse growth. Some branches tried desperately to reach upward but the majority hung down, unable or willing to elevate themselves; they tried but gave up. There was another stretch of bare bark before the top, before the part of the tree that truly represents where I am headed. The highest part of the tree was lush and green and full.

"That's me, you know," I said to my friend as I pointed to the tree. I described the different sections and what they represented for me. Through tears I pointed to the beautiful canopy at the top just past the last bare section.

"That's what's next," I said. "I'm almost there."

Chapter 26

Change

I thought about you today. Again. It took longer for the tears to come, longer for the pain to surface, longer for the sadness, anger, angst, and frustration to rise. It took longer for me to reach for the phone to verbally vomit on a trusted friend about how I felt in that exact moment. It took longer.

They say, "That's progress."

I recall when you once told me, "Change is hard."

A temperate fall morning, perfect by east coast standards for October. Along the route to my annual breast cancer tournament, I took in the mist rising near the river's edge. I noticed the sun peeking through the trees that were adorned with yellow, orange, and red leaves. I saw the exhaled breath of blanket covered horses in the fields. I felt alive and relished the start of my drive while sipping coffee and immersing myself in the nearby landscape. And then thoughts of you drifted in.

I remembered and reminisced, my mind set to rewind. A little over a year earlier, you came to my area for the first time to watch me play in this same tournament and to meet some of my friends. You came bearing gifts of softball snacks and toys and treats for my cats. I remember how amazing it felt spending time getting to know you better, how you were willing and wanting to see me in my element to be supportive.

On the morning of the tournament last year I drove to your

hotel bearing coffee for you—black. I think we were both a little nervous, like newly dating teenagers, but it still felt good and right. We stopped for more coffee closer to the field, and that's when I met your first grandson on a video chat and wished him happy birthday with you. He was adorable, charming, witty, clearly loves his gram-mom, and certainly not shy.

Last year's wonderful memory twisted itself into a dreaded sadness as I approached that second coffee stop. The beauty around me vanished and became clouded with tears. My heart hurt, my breathing became shallow, and my throat burned. I got off the phone with my friend and collected as much of myself as I could to get myself more coffee.

I was less than ten minutes from the field and had to get my act together. It's never a good idea to play a game that uses bats and balls and not have your head in it! A quick return call to my friend resulted in a pep talk that brought me back to the present moment.

"You're going to have a good time today. Be open to it," she encouraged.

I eeked out an "OK" in response.

And so it went. I was one of the last players of our team to arrive, slightly amused to be playing on a team of women much younger than me but secure enough in my softball abilities to know I'd easily earn my spot—and their admiration. The distraction of catching instead of pitching the first game helped my emotional state tremendously. I felt like I had rebooted. Even though we played in the same park as last year, we were playing in a higher bracket and therefore on different fields, which also helped my focus.

We won the first two games and had a slight break before the third game. My mind wandered again. I remembered seeing you and Cooper Chang's grandmom sitting behind the backstop chatting it up last year—talking teacher stuff, education stuff, as I pitched. I remembered how wonderful it felt to be with someone who appeared so secure and together. I still see your smile and hear your laughter. I remembered the warm flutter I felt whenever our eyes met. I can still easily draw on the blossoming love I felt that weekend. I remembered the response you had for my friends when they asked, "Is she *worth* the three-hour drive?" I remembered how it felt walking across the field to the bathrooms with you—being close, feeling connected in a way I'd never felt. I remembered so much about the details of that amazing weekend as we were learning about each other. I remembered how awesome it felt.

I gasped. I got choked up. The sadness rose. My body trembled. My breathing got shallow. Tears flowed. I found myself lost in the past. Again. It's been nearly two months, two months since you let *me* go via Facebook messenger. It's also been about two weeks since we last messaged, and you wrote to tell me to let *this* go. "What is *this* and what does that mean?" my aching heart asked.

"Change is hard," I heard you say inside my head. "For whom?" was my inner response.

Chapter 27

Thanks Coach!

SCREW YOU!

I didn't have to actually say the words. My defiant teenage body language said them loud and proud, with my slight side slouch, arms folded tightly across my chest, one foot folded back behind me with the top half of my body leaning against the hallway lockers. I'm sure my eyes were sporting a fiery glare that could have burned a hole in steel. I listened as politely as I could, considering the circumstances. *If I allowed the mistreatment a third time, that would be on me. Not THIS time!*

The revered high school coach pulled me out of class to talk at me (yes, *at* me).

"I need you," she said. "I need you at practice today—after school," poking me in the chest with her index finger.

"Yeah? I won't be there," I replied.

"Why not?" Coach asked.

"I'm gonna get a job, make some money." I switched feet.

"Don't be silly. Listen, you're going to be working for the rest of your life. This is your time to play," was the retort.

"Uh huh. OK. We'll see," was my smart-ass teenager response.

"Be there!"

"Nope!" I mumbled under my breath as I returned to class.

~~~

Freshman year I went out for basketball. I wasn't really that good, but I loved the sport. It got me out of the house and gave me something to do for a few hours most days of the week. It felt good to be part of a team, make new friends, and have a purpose outside of "home." Basketball was also a motivating factor in keeping my grades up. If I didn't meet the standards, I was not allowed to participate in extracurricular activities. Those were the school rules.

Coach was disciplined and had rules, too. No smoking, no drinking, no drugs, and if you missed school, the practice before a game or forgot any part of your uniform, you sat the bench on game day; no questions asked. "Rules are rules, and they apply to everyone," she would say. We were also frequently reminded to be good sports and to not embarrass the school, our teammates, or any of the coaches. The rules were clear, concise, reasonable, and applied to everyone. They were also repeated and consistent with *all* the sports under Coach's command.

We were encouraged to pay close attention to the varsity players. "You might learn something," we were told. Some days I enjoyed watching them play more than I enjoyed playing myself. I couldn't stand being scolded from the sidelines if I (or someone else) did something wrong. It doesn't take much to recall memories of the assistant coach smacking her leg with the clipboard in disgust if we messed up or caused a turnover without scoring. That feeling, the feeling of disappointing someone, can still cause me angst. This was supposed to be fun. It was *supposed* to be a welcome break from the same feelings I felt at home. I didn't want to feel like a tin soldier being called to attention. I *wanted* to have fun.

As the season progressed, a couple of junior varsity players actually saw some varsity playtime to gain experience. The varsity coach did this in anticipation of losing several seniors to graduation later that year. Coach would do this near the end of a game that was already pretty much decided or when our team had a hefty lead. I remember one particular game when our varsity team was ahead by more than fifty points. It was ridiculous, a definite embarrassment for the other team. Every single junior varsity player got to go into that game for a few minutes. Every single one except one—me! My grades were fine. I had my complete uniform. I paid attention and did my best. Perhaps it was an oversight or maybe it was deliberate. I will never know. What I do know is how I felt and what I thought. *AM I THAT BAD OF A BASKETBALL PLAYER?*

~~~

Sophomore year I chose to go out for softball. *I've played recreational slow pitch softball for years. I KNOW I'm good at that. How hard can the transition to fast pitch softball be?*

I was about to find out.

The basic game is the same but there are some major differences in base running, hitting, and pitching. In fast pitch you can lead, steal, and run to first base on a dropped third strike. Bunting is also permitted. The mechanics and styles of fast pitch pitching are also very different from slow pitch. In the beginning of the season, everyone starts out equal and gets an opportunity to showcase their talents. In essence, every position was up for grabs.

It's common practice to have backup players in case of injury for the positions that demand an elevated level of skill. These positions are pitcher, catcher, and shortstop in fast pitch. As positions were shaking out, it was clear that another freshman pitcher had more natural talent than I had. Her pitches were equally fast and accurate. She was also able to bat and field her position. Even though I knew I wouldn't see much playtime, I was content to be her backup. After all, I was a team player.

~~~

"Did you hear?"

"Hear what?" I asked.

"She forgot her uniform! It's hanging on the clothesline in her backyard!"

Oh WOW! I'm pitching today!

I went through the school day with an inner smile, knowing that today was *my* day to pitch. *Rules are rules, and they apply to everyone,* I heard in Coach's voice.

I don't remember where the game was that day, but I do know it was "away" and we had to take a school bus. Coach's favorites gathered the team's gear and boarded the bus ahead of the rest of us. The usual back of the bus chatter was already underway when I noticed Coach talking to the bus driver. It didn't take long to realize we were taking a detour; the bus was not immediately heading to the other school. Laughter erupted from the back of the bus as we pulled up to the starting pitcher's house. She jumped out, ran around back, and yanked her uniform off the clothesline! Almost everyone on the bus was laughing hysterically when she returned to the bus and got dressed.

Well, that's pretty effed up! Now what?

I remember being torn. She *was* the better pitcher. I *am* a team player and committed to the season. I *do* play recreational slow pitch softball with several teammates after the high school season. I also didn't want to be seen as a crybaby or poor sport. *This sucks. This really, really sucks.*

After the bus incident I did see some "playtime" in the outfield but hated it. It's not the position I wanted to play. Not today, not tomorrow, not ever. I sucked it up because it was needed, but I certainly didn't like it. Fortunately, the season was over soon enough and I could enjoy myself playing slow pitch rec ball. I had plenty of time to think about what I wanted to do before next season.

Life at home sucked. I was bored in school and had even less interest in going to college. My divorced parents made it known they didn't have the money to get me the braces I needed, much less the money to send me for higher education. Coach had already proved to me twice that she was invested in her college-bound favorites. It was clear I was on my own.

I knew when the first high school softball practice of the season was. As the day approached the feeling of being overlooked by Coach during that blowout basketball game returned. The sound of the laughter on the softball bus echoed in my head from the day Coach was too weak to hold to her own rules—the day she avoided having a tough conversation with me about her blatant disregard. I remembered it well and felt it deeply in my body.

There was no way I was going to put myself out there for more of the same. Twice was more than enough. I really didn't care how revered she was by everyone else. This was small-town high school softball. It was supposed to be about the kids—all of them. I gave that coach more of an explanation than was owed and kept the "SCREW YOU" to myself. I had learned who she was and in time learned so much more about who *I* am.

Fortunately, I was blessed with many amazing recreational coaches after my high school experience. They saw my potential and took the time to cultivate it. Those "less-skilled, recreational coaches" taught me so much about life, sportsmanship, and the importance of consistency—both on and off the field. Much of what I learned from them I still use today.

I'm still grateful for my high school experiences with the revered coach as well. I learned that I'm a bad-ass. I used the anger and frustration I felt back then to catapult myself forward in so many ways. My secret drive to ***prove her wrong*** may have been intensely juvenile but it worked out beautifully for me!

I retired from full-time work over ten years ago at the

tender age of forty-eight; so much for working for the rest of my life! I *also* still play softball competitively with women in their twenties and thirties! In 2022 I pitched the championship game in the senior Olympics--my team took the gold! The following year I competed in Winter Worlds in Myrtle Beach, South Carolina, AND the Challenge Cup at the USSSA Space Coast Complex in Melbourne , Florida!

Amazing accomplishments for a high school bench warmer now pushing sixty!

Thanks Coach!

Chapter 28

A Magical Moment in Time

From a distance my eyes zeroed in on the small, blue pet carrier before I noticed anything else. *I wonder if there's anything in it.* I widened my field of vision and saw that it was being carried in a woman's right hand. There was another woman present with a man next to her. They were standing on the paver-laced sidewalk next to a parked car with its rear passenger door open. As I approached I saw white and black fur through the holes in the carrier's side. I did what I normally do: I ignored the people and addressed the critter.

"Oh hey, who's going for a ride?" I asked.

The woman spun the carrier around, and I was immediately drawn to its contents. Inside was an incredibly handsome, docile, and "knowing" cat. What he "knew" I did not yet know. What I did know was how powerful his energy was. He grabbed *my* attention and held it. When I get that feeling, I know to pay attention, that something really wonderful is going to show up or happen.

Eventually, I spoke with the cat's people. I commented on how cool and good-looking their cat was. We made small talk, and I lingered just long enough to see if the cat or the people had more information for me—but not so long that they'd think I was some kind of creeper. *Time to move on,* I heard inside my head and did.

~~~

Since COVID, healers worldwide have been uniting daily

on ZOOM calls. Individually and collectively, we gather to amplify and use our spiritual gifts on ourselves, others, and the planet. On many of the calls we offer up prayers and healing for those who are experiencing difficult situations. In the beginning I was very eager and paid close attention to each of the requests and sent out love and light exponentially. Over time I found myself distracted on many of the calls because events in my own life had become a sh*t show. Some days I found myself wallowing in self-pity and not having any f*cks to give. In essence, I was "on" the calls but not really a willing participant. I was half-listening because it was the very best I could do.

Recently, I partially heard about a baby with medical challenges. Halfheartedly, I picked up pieces of the baby's story over time. There was an unhealed piece deep inside of me that was jealous of that precious soul, jealous of all the love, care, and concern that was being directed this baby's way. *Why couldn't I have any of that growing up?* I felt those words deep inside my being. They stung.

Days later it was announced there was no more to be done medically so the decision was made to take her off life support, that it was in God's hand now. I *heard* the words but was numb to actually *feeling* them. I was absent from a couple of calls due to a sore back and therefore missed the call detailing when she had actually transitioned.

"The funeral's tomorrow. Please hold 'Baby L' and her family in your thoughts and prayers."

Suddenly, I felt my heart open. "Butterfly" I said tearfully. "Watch for the butterfly. It's not butterfly season so it may not be an actual butterfly. It may be on a card, in a flower arrangement, or on someone's clothes but watch for it! That's her!"

Our support call ended. I went on about my day and forgot all about it until today.

~~~

I smiled inside at the brief experience with the cat. *I don't know what that was all about, but it sure grabbed my attention.* A few steps later I froze in disbelief. If I were walking at my regular pace or distracted with my usual thoughts, I'd have walked right past it.

I stopped and took a picture to send to my healer friend. She was likely "at" or on her way to "Baby L's" services. There it was. Under the back end of a parked car, just behind the rear wheel, likely another kid's school art project, a home-made butterfly! An undeniable sign from "Baby L." She had arrived safely at her "other world."

Grateful doesn't adequately describe the feeling of being able to bring this kind of comfort to a grieving family. It's indescribable. It DOES make me feel like I have a purpose, though. It empowers me and gives me hope for my own future.

The destination for this walk was my coffee place. I looked up to see the "cat carrying people" at the end of the line.

"How'd you guys beat me here?" I asked.

The woman turned, laughed, and said, "Nice to see you again." Then, for some unknown reason, she showed me a picture of her other cat while we waited. This second encounter felt weird, not creepy weird, just "get my attention" weird.

When I started to leave the coffee place, I felt something passing through me. Instinctively, I knew it was "Baby L." *I'm here, baby girl,* I heard inside my head. *Is there a message?* Her message was simply, "Thank you, thank you for loving me the way all things should be loved." I immediately dialed my friend and tearfully relayed the message to her voicemail.

I literally felt "Baby L" pass through me. She was warm and giggly. Her energy was light, joyful, and free. I felt honored to give her a voice and feel her innocent presence. Before leaving she shared the incredible love and light she was in. The feeling was amazing—truly, a magical moment in time.

What a lucky baby! To have and be able to feel so much love and support even if for such a short time. To truly know who you are and your purpose in this lifetime. WOW, just WOW.

The experience changed me. Something inside me shifted. I didn't feel resentful or jealous of "Baby L." Absent were the selfish and bitter feelings that somebody else had something "better" than me, that lousy "not good enough, not deserving" feeling that plagued so much of my life. In THIS magical moment I had gratitude. I had an immense gratitude to "Baby L" for sharing selflessly. However brief the moment, I was present to experience and witness and truly *feel deeply* what it was like to have what my heart always knew was possible.

Many spiritual teachings state, "Gratitude opens the heart." I was about to find out just how true that statement is. I went on with my chores and my day, including writing this chapter. I thought it was complete a few paragraphs ago. I was sooo, sooo mistaken.

I had had enough of chores and took a drive with a friend to Peddler's Village in New Hope. There are great opportunities for walking, shopping, eating, and people watching. We walked into the first store: butterflies! Butterflies at the entrance, butterfly mobiles hanging from the ceiling, butterflies on art and clothing, dozens of them! Next store same thing! I laughed and felt loved.

We stopped at a diner on the way home. The energy of the diner was interesting. I couldn't put my finger on it right away. My friend told me to look around. You guessed it! More butterfly art! On the back wall of the diner was a painting of a magical looking lady with bright eyes and a big smile with a butterfly on her left shoulder. *WOW! Is "Baby L" camped out on my left shoulder? Is THAT the message for ME?*

The magic continued.

Chapter 29
More Magic

I started the next day like I start most days. I walked to my favorite spot for finding coins, found sixty cents, and then proceeded to my regular coffee shop. It was an unseasonably warm day for February, and the sun shined brightly—perfect for a Sunday morning walk.

After getting my coffee I spied a lone dollar bill in the mulch, flanked by two short hedges, and giggled like a child. I tucked it in my back pocket and continued walking north on Main. I noticed something unusual about a block away. There was a guy shaking crumbs out onto the sidewalk from a bag of chips or something. My initial reaction was, "What the heck? Who does that? There's a trash can RIGHT THERE!"

Settle down, Sherri. Things aren't always what they seem. Take a breath. Just watch.

The tension and frustration that started to rise in my body had nowhere to go and fizzled before gaining any traction. *The healthier life skills really do work when you remember to use them.* It felt good NOT to judge and be reactive!

I continued walking toward the man. We met in the crosswalk and started to chat.

"There they go!" he said, "Hear that?"

Birds stationed at the top of a nearby tree started singing. The winter-naked branches were at the forefront of a sunshine filled blue sky that held about three dozen or so happy sparrows. I would soon learn they were thanking the man for breakfast.

"It's OK, you're safe. Come on down," the man assured.

And they did.

We chitchatted about the lack of winter, and before we departed the man placed his hand on my forehead and blessed me. The gesture from someone I had literally just met in the middle of a crosswalk was simultaneously strange and normal. For me, it was actually closer to normal.

That was weird. Oh well, I'll take whatever blessings anyone wants to offer.

"I'll cross here so I don't disturb the birds having breakfast," I said to the man as I left him and did. In less than a minute, I discovered the normalcy of the encounter. It got my attention, slowed me down, and essentially guided me to change course.

Crossing the street where I hadn't actually planned to put me on the block where the homemade butterfly was *yesterday* during the time when Main Street was riddled with parked cars. In the stillness of a Sunday morning and completely absent of cars, the child's abandoned art project boldly broadcast its presence near the curb. I lovingly picked it up.

Cross back over Main at the next corner.

I shook my head at the thought of the zigzag route I was taking home but followed the guidance I was being given. *There's a reason. Just go with it!*

I approached the corner near the local funeral home and looked up the driveway. I saw a friend getting out of her car. I walked over to say hello and jokingly asked if I could borrow the hearse to take camping. "It'd be perfect for rolling my kayak in and out of the back."

We laughed. She noticed the butterfly so I explained briefly.

We wished each other a good day and went our own ways. I rounded the corner of the building and was guided to look down. There they were. Two single dollar bills, side-by-side, folded in a way that resembled the wings of yet another butterfly. I stood for a moment and reflected on the divine timing, guidance, and events that led up to this moment. I was awestruck.

Once back home I did a few things and decided on a second walk and coffee.

Follow your internal guidance.

I left the coffee shop, and my "spiritual GPS" sent me home a different route. I listened. I paid very close attention to my surroundings while I walked. For some unknown reason I strolled on the road's edge instead of using the sidewalk. A dirty, twisted piece of paper rested on the section of grass between the curb and sidewalk. I looked down in disbelief. The way it was laid out loosely resembled yet another butterfly. And this one was a ten-dollar bill! "OK. OK. I get it now!"

Change, healing, and transformation are hard. They take courage and time to unravel. Learn from the butterfly's process— there's a time to crawl, to be still, to fly, and to be beautiful. Be present, patient, and kind with yourself during the process.

Chapter 30
Christmas Trigger

I cried myself to sleep last night. Again. The support group I've been going to for a little over three months warned me this would happen. They said I'd move out of denial and begin to start grieving the childhood I lost living with alcoholism and dysfunction. At last night's meeting I was reminded that it never really goes away; that in time I'd just learn to recognize it and use the tools to manage it better and faster.

It's December 2022.

I love winter. The cold is familiar. So is the darkness, quiet, and isolation. *I'll enjoy winter even more once Christmas has passed.* I have silently hated the days leading up to Christmas for the better part of my life. Those pre-holiday days start spinning a movie reel of memories that lead me down a path I've often traveled solo and silently. Sure, there were some that I would classify as "good" but, for longer than I care to admit, I've felt pressured to "celebrate" the holidays in a way that's not consistent with how I really feel.

The deeply embedded and dysfunctional social conditioning I received as a child was to be quiet, be polite, behave, don't ask anyone for anything, and be everything everyone else wanted me to be *or* suffer the consequences with a "good" beating. That's a tall order for a kid on any day, much less the days leading up to a holiday that asks if you were "good" all year. *Of* *course, I was good; I'd get the sh*t beaten out of me even when I was!*

Knowing this time of year can be hard for me, I am living each day one moment at a time and giving myself the care, love, and grace absent from my childhood. I am actively using the tools learned in my Adult Children of Alcoholics and Dysfunction® support group. The program acronym HALT has been especially helpful. It has kept me grounded and given me permission to take care of myself *FIRST and UNAPOLOGETICALLY!* If I am Hungry, Angry, Lonely, or Tired, as the acronym says, I can stop whatever I'm doing and address those needs BEFORE anything or anyone else. This incredibly simple life skill is in stark contrast to what has been demanded of me by evil looks for far too long!

~~~

Yesterday started like any other day. I cared for the cats, took my vitamins, got dressed, and went out for my morning coffee and walk. I participated in daily ZOOM calls, ate breakfast, and felt good enough to hit the gym. I ministered to a friend who lost their niece to suicide, then had a noon recovery meeting. In the afternoon I puttered around the house and celebrated the tiniest progress on projects that had previously become stagnant. I felt good about taking care of myself *and* taking time to listen to the friend that was hurting. My day so far felt balanced and calm.

The program groups have already taught me so much. I have learned to celebrate and share the things that are "working." I am developing greater confidence by asking questions and pre-planning for situations that may make me feel uncomfortable, used, manipulated, or triggered. It felt amazing to take the time yesterday to clarify whether a lunch I was invited to later in the week was "just a lunch" OR a "Christmas lunch." Having this type of information allows me to make better choices and participate in life events in a way that aligns with how I'm feeling in that moment. The new skills have become a large part of my recovery from a life riddled with dysfunction. I have also learned that I can change my mind at any given time. *WOW, what a concept! I can really do that?*

Today was trucking along nicely. I was hardly affected by the plumber needing to reschedule for a second time, and then the mail arrived. Holiday cards from friends were welcome. Holiday cards from clients, nonprofits, and the few cousins that truly make an effort to stay connected were also welcome. The obligatory "look at me and my perfect family" holiday postcard from the bullying and emotionally dismissive, Bible-toting matriarchal cousin was triggering.

I paused. I went within. I remembered my program and the tools I've developed in recovery. I lovingly glanced at my second and third cousins in the picture—they see, respect, and appreciate me. *I'm in touch with them on social media. I see their pictures other places. Does this card bring me joy? Does it get to stay in my house on display with the others that DO bring me joy? NOPE!* I trashed it and called a program friend. She was SO encouraging!

"Good for you! That's progress! Maybe next year you'll skip a step and not even open it!" *Let's hope!*

Unraveling takes time, patience, courage, and the support of people who get it or at least have the capacity to truly try and understand. It was important for me to get to a meeting, and I did. I am grateful for the fellowship and being in the presence of others on a similar journey. That doesn't mean the sadness, triggers, and toxic thoughts magically vanish, but it does mean that I can progress by feeling truly heard and supported. I can be around fellow travelers walking a path that resembles mine. That feels so much better than having my emotional pains denied, diluted, or dismissed!

I have learned to check in with myself frequently. I have

grasped the concept of lovingly tending to those parts of me that are still hurting. I now understand that unraveling is an opportunity to re-parent myself and reclaim those parts of me that were repeatedly beaten into submission and radical compliance. Last night was one of those nights.

As I put my head on the pillow, I felt a sadness within me rise. I let it. Tears followed. I surrendered to the experience without judgment, without trying to hold back or make sense of it. I observed it. Feeling this tired, sad, and alone reminded me of a Christmas Eve a very long time ago.

I was the only child in a cigarette smoke filled house with red, plush wall-to-wall carpeting in the large living room. Dinner was long over, and the small kitchen was a disaster. *I'm Dreaming of a White Christmas* was playing from the walnut brown stereo console in the background; a burning, lone cigarette rested in an astray above the right speaker. All the adults were laughing and drinking. I was bored, tired, and just wanted to go to sleep. One bedroom was off-limits because of unwrapped presents, and the other held everyone's smelly coats; some reeked of men's aftershave or cologne, some of cheap, old lady perfume, and others of stale smoke.

I remembered begging and pleading with my half-sauced mother to just take me home—less than a five-minute drive. I didn't even care if she left me home alone and went back. I remember being so tired that Christmas Eve that I just wanted to cry. I also know that if I embarrassed her by crying I was in for a good beating. In that old memory I felt hopeless and helpless.

In last night's memory I snuggled with my inner child as I imagined re-parenting myself. Last night I gave little Sherri what she really needed and deserved growing up. In my new memory I kissed her on the head and reassured her. *It's OK, sweetie, I'm here now, I've got you.* I soon stopped crying and drifted off to sleep effortlessly.

On my morning's walk I recalled how the previous night ended. *Can re-parenting myself really be that simple?* My answer came almost immediately in coins: three quarters and a dime. The silver coins totaled eighty-five, the year my birth mother died. Another pivotal unraveling moment indeed.

UPDATE: I read the draft of this story to a program friend a few days later and followed that call up with a head-clearing walk. I found forty-nine cents on that walk—the age of my mother at her death. Two days later I found coins that represented the month and day of *my* birth. I have decided to use today as my *new* birthday and am giving myself the love and care I always knew I deserved.

Chapter 31

Morning Magic

Curious by nature, I have always wanted to know why things are the way they are. I've asked questions inside my head for a really long time. I *had* to ask them there because I'd get yelled at for asking too many or laughed at if my question was "stupid." I know now that some of my "stupid" questions were just classified that way because the person I'd asked was embarrassed for not knowing the answer or ashamed by the truth. They'd avoid or deflect. For the longest time I thought I was crazy—until I realized I wasn't.

The truth is that unhealthy people are avoidant. I learned that particular method of communication from my family of origin; sadly, it has played out over and over through the course of my life. It's played out in friendships, partnerships, and work relationships. The one thing it's taught me is to be a better listener and to pay attention to what's not being said. I've also learned to ask more questions—either out loud when I feel safe with the person I am talking with or in the stillness of my own mind when I do not.

I've been asking a lot of questions inside my head lately. *Why do I feel the way I do? Why do I feel so unworthy? When did that start? Why can't I finish things? What's next for me? Where do I want to go? What do I want to do?* My favorite time to ask is in the quiet of the morning—during my search for coins on the way for coffee. Most times the coins I find give me answers and direction.

Lower back and hip pain have plagued me on and off for the better part of my adult life. I've done chiropractic, physical therapy, massage, heat, cold, acupressure, and several other alternative therapies. I've found relief of varying duration with each modality but know in my gut the underlying cause is not physical. As I peel away the layers of the onion and follow the divine guidance I'm given, I'm learning that much of what I feel isn't even mine; in many cases the really intense feelings belong to my ancestors! I've been so hell-bent on moving forward and healing from my own stuff that I have been clueless about so much of the crap that came before I was even a glimmer of a thought!

Divine guidance led me to a twelve-step recovery program to deal with the fallout from growing up in an alcoholic and dysfunctional home. It has also placed several books, people, and resources in my path so I can reclaim all that was stolen or absent from my childhood. In *It Didn't Start With You*, the author explains how our cells can hold up to three generations of information.

Holy Sh*t! I'm carrying around baggage that doesn't even belong to me—from people I've never even met or heard of. What in the hell am I supposed to do with that now?

I *thought* my mother's anger was survivor's guilt, guilt from surviving polio when her teenage brother perished from it. My family didn't talk about things, and I'd get yelled at for asking so I didn't. That left plenty of holes in my history. *How can I possibly heal myself when I don't even know what I need to know to heal it?*

I went out for my morning walk as I held these thoughts. More questions came up. More thoughts. *What was Mom's relationship with her brother like? I don't ever remember hearing her talk about him. Was it abusive like mine with my sibling? Did she miss him? What was the family dynamic like before he died? Was that when Gramps started drinking? Is that what led to Gramps and Gram splitting up? Everybody's dead so how can I get answers? And crap, I don't know ANYTHING about Dad's side other than that ALL his brothers drank; one even owned a liquor store at one point.*

And then it hit me. It's time to do another family constellation process, maybe two. One for Mom's side and one for Dad's. As I held the thought of whose side I should do first, I went about my walk. My answer came quickly. Forty-nine coins. The age my mother was when she suffered a fatal heart attack.

My next step was decided.

Chapter 32
Family Constellation

"I do believe in spooks, I do believe in spooks, I do, I do, I do."

The cowardly lion from *The Wizard of Oz* repeated in my head as I planned my third family constellation process. Taking this trip with a trusted therapist and complete strangers took courage, strength, and a commitment to healing. *What will I learn this time?*

~~~

Family constellation therapy is a therapeutic intervention used to gain insight and information into a client's family history, dynamics, and possible dysfunctional patterns. Developed by German therapist Bert Hellinger, it is based on components of Gestalt therapy and psycho-dynamic therapy.

When employing the family constellation, the therapist has people unrelated to the client stand in as the various family members who then act out the dynamics related to the individual's concerns. The technique is considered a form of "expressive therapy," and the goal is to assist in working through concerns or to develop better insight.

~~~

Since this was my third constellation since 2016, I knew what was expected of me and was prepared to just dive in and get started. I don't know that I went into this one wanting answers so much as confirmation to what I *thought* I knew was the truth.

We met on ZOOM. The participants were introduced, and everyone was briefed on the process and order of events. I needed answers to family dynamics that had taken place long before I was even a thought. I had to understand.

I chose people to "stand in" for the major players of the constellation—Grandma, Gramps, my mom, Mom's dead brother, the male foster kid that I felt was a "replacement" for Mom's brother that died, me, and my sibling (even though neither of us were even born yet).

The backstory and goal of the session were explained to the participants.

Mom and Uncle Teddy were teenagers when they both contracted polio. A newspaper article said the cause of Teddy's death was polio. However, several years ago someone familiar with my family insisted he drowned. I KNOW Mom and Grandma were terrified of the water and never learned to swim. Is that because Teddy really drowned?

Sometime after Teddy died Grandma started taking in babies to foster; all but one were male. Was she trying to replace Teddy over and over again? What was she thinking or feeling? Did she consider my mother's feelings? How did my mother feel about all this? I often thought my mother suffered from survivor's guilt. Is that what happened? Or was it something else? Is the loss of Teddy what drove my gramps to drinking that led to their eventual divorce?

The facilitator created a safe, energetic container for the process to unfold. Almost immediately, the players began to speak. I don't remember the dialogue verbatim but I do recall feeling a lot of confusion, hurt, guilt, anger, and angst being unraveled before me. I witnessed complete chaos unraveling. *These people couldn't figure out how to get out of a ripped paper bag together.* From this spiritual vantage point, I was able to compassionately connect with everyone's position individually but still needed answers to my own personal suffering. I *know* it didn't start with me but it will most definitely end with me.

Uncle Teddy was the golden child. He was the glue that held the family together. When he died the family unit fractured. Gramps started drinking, Grandma took in her first foster baby, a boy, and my mom became invisible. Over time Mom's invisibility turned inward to rage, self-hatred, and a lack of self-esteem. She passed those traits down and physically took her rage out on me. *Did I somehow represent that foster baby boy that took her place in the family when she was just a teen?*

But there was more. The facilitator alluded to a big, fat, family secret, suggesting that the family I thought was my family might not really be and that I stop digging.

"It's possible that your mother may not have been born to the woman you know as your grandmother," he said.

Not much more I can do with this. I've unraveled enough chaos here. Time to let this string go. I've reached its frayed and tattered end.

Chapter 33

Trauma, Triggers, and Truth

Unlike the loosely crocheted stitch in the afghan from Chapter 1, my triggers and trauma were woven together so tightly they formed a noose that strangled and stunted my truth and growth. The dichotomy of what I was taught as a youngster versus my inner knowledge had me questioning so many things for far too long. Wanting to believe and belong and not wanting to disagree or disappoint left me silently feeling less than, incredibly inadequate, and sometimes even thinking *I* was the crazy one. My truth back then WAS my triggers and trauma. They were all I knew, and they were one. Impervious.

My UNraveling has taken much patience and persistence. I found that playing tug-of-war with myself only tightened the rope. At some point I dropped the rope, and the fibers loosened. I became so much clearer about whether something was a trigger, related to a trauma, or my actual truth. I learned to pay close attention to my own words and how I felt inside. If I started to sound like I was telling a story or defending a course of action or spending too much time rationalizing, I knew to just stop and sit with the situation. I've learned through much trial and error that that's how emotionally healthy adults do it. I don't have to overthink it *or* get anyone to agree with me. Sure, I will occasionally bounce things off of trusted friends but I no longer feel the incredible urge to convince anyone of my choices or defend them.

I recently agonized for far longer than I should have about an upcoming trip. There were many aspects of the trip that made me incredibly uncomfortable. Determined to do it differently, I did my due diligence and asked questions—lots of them. Prior to making the second payment installment, I asked the travel consultant for the contact information of the person I was paired up with. We were going to be sharing close quarters on a private yacht for several days, and I had every right to decide for myself if it was going to work.

Today when I'm troubled, I stop and ask myself, "Who is talking? Is this a trigger, trauma or truth?" Sometimes it's a combination, and sometimes I have to ask more than once for clarity. I have friends I can ask to "check me."

Chapter 34

More Than a Chapter

"I don't want to be *just* another chapter in one of your books," she said.

She wasn't.

One of my biggest teachers, she taught me about love, laughter, life, and learning. She also sent me further back and deeper into my healing than anyone before. Her presence and participation in my life also lifted me higher than most. She saw into me. She wasn't afraid of my history.

My "Jersey directness" may have frightened her at first, but she countered it by nurturing and encouraging my soft side. I also began to enjoy some of the things I had previously found triggering such as holidays, family gatherings, kids' sporting events, and painfully long piano recitals. With her, I started to open up again. I looked forward to a Labor Day picnic that I was invited (and subsequently UNinvited) to just before the keyboard coward "let me go." Conversely, the canyon left after her sudden, unexpected departure caused disruptions to every single layer of my being.

Among the first physical eruptions was a mysterious lump under my left ear. It felt hot and itchy as it increased in size daily during a cycle of antibiotics. It also refilled quickly after being drained and biopsied. In between follow-up visits it eventually burst, shriveled up, and disappeared, rather like our relationship.

Soon after muscle tightness, weakness, unexplained fatigue, lower back pain, and a twisted pelvis severely hampered my mobility. A huge chunk of tooth number eighteen cracked off to the point where it was no match for a filling and required a root canal and crown.

Each of the maladies had their own spiritual message for me, and none of them felt good, especially not the root canal. After raising my hand twice for more Novocain, I swore the dentist's drill bit was going to exit the bottom of my jaw. *Those were some deeply embedded beliefs!*

Subsequently, the permanent crown didn't sit properly, and a cavity appeared in the tooth next to it. The plan was to address the cavity and create a new mold for the crown on my next visit. A softball injury delayed sitting in the dentist's chair for several weeks. No telling when I will reschedule. A year after the breakup, I was still searching for answers and pain relief for the physical and emotional traumas that the fainthearted breakup triggered. It's not been easy.

The physical pain sidelined daily activities, forcing me to "sit with" what I've unconsciously avoided for much of my adult life. Repressed emotions were wreaking havoc on my body and its systems. I halfheartedly walked the path of conventional medicine despite knowing with ninety-nine percent certainty that the "root" cause of my physical symptoms was emotional. They were a tightly bound ball of repressed, suppressed, unexpressed, and current emotions. And they sucked. What sucked even more was not being able to do the things I normally did to find relief. No river guiding. No kayaking. No hiking. No gym. And I was praying for rain on softball days because jolts of pain shot through the left side of my body with nearly every step.

But I read, wrote, landed in Adult Children of Alcoholics and Dysfunction® (ACA®), and listened.

And learned.

I read and learned about attachment theory, how to get the love I want, trauma, boundaries, co-dependence, love bombing, para-alcoholism, enmeshment, enabling versus helping, healthy relationships and behavior, active listening, trauma bonds, people pleasing, fixers, twin flames, family roles, how to recognize under- and over-functioning individuals, addictions of all kinds, emotionally immature parents, the source of all this crazy, and, most importantly, how to navigate, feel, and begin to recover from all of it. I listened to a book on resilience and healing, began attending ACA® meetings with regular frequency, and started to treat myself to the grace, love, and understanding I craved and deserve. Slowly, and with purpose, I took real charge of my recovery.

And now I can thank her.

The Teacher. The mother who birthed my latest round of pain and suffering.

Intense feelings of being abandoned by her and everyone else have temporarily subsided. Similar to the tide, they rise and fall. Contrary to the tide, raw emotions don't surface gracefully on a predictable schedule. Oh no, they come barging in unannounced, without warning like an unexpected storm. I now know the rejection seed was planted early in childhood and fertilized by the lifelong cycles of crazy and chaos that were my familiars. ACA® teachings* explore the intense and sometimes unreasonable fear of abandonment developed in our earliest years. I now understand how my distorted worldview had me clinging desperately to unhealthy people, situations, and relationships to sidestep the discomfort of feeling abandoned by anyone and everyone. How giving in or rolling with a situation just to avoid conflict is another unhealthy behavior beaten into me as a child. Truthfully, whenever I act with the sole purpose of easing another person's discomfort, I abandon myself. Also it limits that other person's opportunity for expansion, keeping *them* stuck. The opposite of a win-win, it's a lose-lose.

My physical pain intensified. A month of chiropractic care to find the pain source was more like a game of whack-a-mole. It morphed from lower back pain to a twisted pelvis to bad shoes, piriformis syndrome, sciatica, a pinched nerve, something between L3 and L4 to something between L4 and L5, and on and on. I rested. I was adjusted, muscle tested, stretched, put in traction, and had ultrasound with various liniments and tinctures including, of all things, one used for horses! I even had my left glute pounded with a handheld massager that felt like a rubber jackhammer. After many visits and continued suffering, I decided to try physical therapy. A month into that resulted in much of the same.

I know this is emotional. I KNOW my body is trying to tell me something. How do I get to the root?

~~~

I just wanted to cry and maybe even die. *THIS* was not living. *THIS* was not good. I *KNOW* the connection between emotions and the body. *THIS* went beyond my understanding and comprehension. A program friend suggested *The Mindbody Prescription: Healing the Body, Healing the Pain* by John E. Sarno, MD. Subsequently, I stumbled on the works of Gabor Maté. As I unraveled my emotions and pain, I dove deep into the study of where they started. With normal vital signs and another discussion with my primary physician about the possibility of Tension Myositis Syndrome (TMS), XRAYS, blood work, and an MRI were ordered just before going to print.

~~~

Initially, I felt like a broken oscillating fan stuck in the direction of grief, sadness, loneliness, isolation, and abandonment. My chest was heavy, and sometimes I had to remind myself to breathe. Occasionally, my "feeling fan" would start to swing slowly in the other direction, then quickly ricochet back to woe. Even the radio was a source of angst since nearly every single song reminded me of her— reminded me of how I would tell her house voice command system to play something soothing to help her go to sleep every night. That is, every night until two additional adults, dogs, and reptiles moved into her house. Our intimate nighttime calls changed. The "adults" in the next bedroom monkeyed with the voice command system, turning her bedroom light into more of a strobe during our calls. Slightly muffled evil laughter in the background followed. Sometimes I'd be muted after hearing a knock on her closed bedroom door. Sometimes I'd be talking but not knowing there was someone else in the room. I missed our private conversations and the loving smile each night's song choice would display as she drifted off to sleep during our nightly video chats.

I could almost hear the fan click as it tried to move in the opposite direction. Feelings stuck remembering the early months of our relationship. I remembered so many details and missed so much of our time together. I missed all her different smiles, laughs, and mannerisms; the way she shook her leg when she was nervous, the different inflections in her voice that told me how tickled (or annoyed) she was with something. Dancing in the kitchen. The way she pronounced certain words like sandwich and the adorable nickname she gave me early on. The nickname that was lovingly bedazzled onto a nightshirt that matched a cute pair of buffalo plaid pajama shorts.

"Everybody in the family gets PJs for Christmas," she said.

"It takes time," I kept hearing.

Our time before the adult children moved back in was amazing. It was fun, loving, and adventurous; almost too easy. I wanted this to work so badly that I missed, poo-pooed, or was completely unaware of the early red flags. The attention, affection, cards, and poems were very welcome but the overabundance of food and gifts made me uncomfortable. I thought about how discussing my discomfort was rejected and resulted in much of the same behavior. How my first birthday present wasn't just one blanket but two. These were nice gestures, and I thanked her despite also voicing that I'm not a "things" person and that I'm more of a "spending quality time and having new experiences" kind of person. I secretly wondered if I was being ungrateful or unreasonable. I know I'm a better giver than receiver. *Maybe this is something I need to learn and accept. Other people like gifts, what's wrong with me?* (I hadn't yet learned the term "love bombing.") Oh, the irony of Mom's handmade afghans and my girlfriend's gift of blankets. Well-intentioned gifts of love, I'm sure, but it's impossible to give what you don't have for yourself.

I dismissed the overabundance of calls and video chats to and from her one adult child when we were together. *They're just really close,* I thought to myself. I dismissed that first video chat with her adult child the day of *our* introductory in-person meeting. How my lighthearted "it was nice to meet you but you're on my time with your mom," was met with the response of "It's ALL my time." I later learned I wasn't the first suitor to make a comment like that.

I also ignored the discomfort I felt the first time I met the eldest and their spouse. One threatened to kill me, and the spouse said they knew where to hide my body. I learned they were trying to be funny by quoting a movie. A movie I had never seen. The "joke" fell flat. It was uncomfortable for me. My new girlfriend, visibly nervous by the exchange and my response to it, did her best to play it off as a joke.

Further, I completely hid my displeasure with the nickname "Chit" that was given to me by my girlfriend's firstborn. *They just want you to like them.* It was supposed to be short for "Chicken Shit" because I wouldn't repeat a missed comment during another one of our three-way conversations. I later learned that the word chit has several derogatory meanings in the Urban Dictionary. In retrospect, I feel it was a subtle way for the adult child to appear cutesy when they were really just being a bully. Unconsciously desperate to "fit in," I willingly took part in a chicken themed birthday celebration for that adult child complete with a silly chicken children's game and chick figurine for the cake. Suffice it to say, connecting with my girlfriend this way felt good. Our good time, laughter, and displays of genuine affection for each other came with a price, though. I believe that was the day jealousy was born. The day there was an angry yank on the nearly forty-year-old umbilical cord.

Then that couple moved in—temporarily.

My gut was giving me information but I was slow to understand it. At the time I thought I was being patient, kind, and understanding. I had set a boundary that I wouldn't stay at her house while they were there; the arrangement was temporary after all. She'd come to me or we'd travel together or meet halfway. I did negotiate the boundary *once* for an overnight to attend a party. The event was important to her, and I wanted to show my support. *It's only one night. I can do this for her.*

She said her adult child just wanted me to like them and was excited to make omelets for breakfast. The morning came, and there was a knock at our bedroom door.

"We have to leave soon. I cooked the veggies and sausage. Can you make the omelets?"

The night before three of us were watching TV, and I felt like I was being glared at by a self-appointed chaperone. *Who is the parent here?* The overnight stay was awkward.

She *said* she wanted me to advocate for myself but, in

reality, there were topics that really pushed her buttons. I found myself between a rock and a hard place. If I asked about a certain someone, I was "being nosy and judging," and if I didn't ask, I didn't care. That's really tough to navigate.

In time more of *her* time was being consumed by others and other activities and less time was spent on "us" and our relationship. It felt like our calls and video chats were constantly being interrupted or monitored by a needy child saying "Mommy, look at me." Emotional flashbacks of age-appropriate behavior attempting to get MY own mother's attention as a youngster surfaced. I was frustrated, and I suspect she started to feel it. At one point I actually thought I was being unreasonable and asking for too much. After checking in with friends and a therapist, I was assured that requesting time for private conversations, vacations, and video chats with my girlfriend was absolutely within healthy limits. I felt reassured while doing my best to be sensitive to her "temporary" situation.

Time spent with her other adult child and their family felt much less threatening. We met at their kids' sporting events and a piano recital. Besides the recital being painfully long, I really enjoyed spending time with them. I looked forward to the picnic and getting to know that side of the family better. Saying so was clearly triggering to my girlfriend, and I was subsequently UNinvited. She gave me two excuses. The first was how my NOT staying overnight would be interpreted by the adult child staying with her. The second was because inappropriate behavior by a previous girlfriend was being unfairly projected onto me. *If I didn't push back after my life was threatened, it's safe to say I'd know how to conduct myself at a picnic.* I believed the initial reason was the *real* reason. My sense was that my girlfriend was trying to oversee *my choice* of where to stay in an effort to manage her eldest adult child's feelings. Feelings that are really not hers to manage.

I could *feel* the anxiety of the situation causing her internal panic. She was withdrawing. It felt crazy yet familiar; like trying to keep a moth from bouncing off a hot light bulb. My feelings were also crazy. I cared deeply and hated knowing she was struggling. I *wanted* to help her but stayed in my own lane. It was not mine to navigate, fix, or feel. I resolved to cheering silently and hoped she would find herself and her voice and ask for what she needed— from everyone.

I wanted her to want more for herself. I wanted *her* to see that she is amazing *and* lovable. She is worthy and deserving of love *without* having to dance around or manage everyone else's feelings.

She was much more than a chapter. She was an amazing teacher.

And I am grateful.

*ACA® Laundry List, The Other Laundry List and The Problem.

Chapter 35

The Race to Love

"YOU'RE A RACIST!"

"WHAT DID YOU CALL ME?"

"YOU HEARD ME! YOU'RE A RACIST!"

I was walking up the street to meet friends for my town's annual Memorial Day parade. It's hard to describe in words exactly how I was feeling in that moment because I was doing my best to keep myself moving from an intensely emotional week. There was a woman walking toward me. She stopped to let her dog crap on someone's lawn. Her back was to the dog while she carried on a conversation with a guy across the street. They were both walking in the same direction.

The dog finished. She and the guy were still walking and talking. I was in my own head and said nothing as we passed. It was unusual for me NOT to attempt to make eye contact, say hello, or at least acknowledge the dog. As I passed the spot where the dog "went," I saw it was loose.

"Hey," I yelled back in the woman's direction. "Your dog has the runs."

She turned back to face me. "YOU'RE A RACIST!"

"WHAT DID YOU CALL ME?" I shouted back.

"YOU HEARD ME! YOU'RE A RACIST!"

This world has gone freaking bonkers. ME? RACIST? This shit has got to stop. I have been called all kinds of things, mostly by my twisted sibling, but I have NEVER been called a racist. I won't allow it! Not without an explanation!

I furiously and expeditiously spun my whole body around like Linda Blair spun her head in *The Exorcist* and squared up to face her. In that moment, raw from the week's events of losing a dear friend and more emotional turmoil and upheaval than anyone should have to face in an entire lifetime, I was NOT about to let this unwarranted name calling pass. No, not this time. I have blown off other's bad behavior and mistreatment too many times in the fifty-eight years I've walked this earth. It stops right here! Right now!

We walked toward each other. I lowered my voice some since we were getting closer to one another. "Are you effing kidding me? Please tell me how my concern for YOUR dog's health translates into ME being a racist! That's a pretty big leap."

She angrily waved a roll of poop bags in the air, asking how I expected her to clean up liquid. I continued walking toward her.

"Lady, I'm letting you know your dog has diarrhea. I'm concerned for your dog's health. How in the hell does that make me racist? Tell me! I want to know." I pressed as we got even closer.

"You pass me all the time. You say hi to the dogs and not me. You disrespect me, you racist."

I leaned in closer. Fearless. This woman was no threat to me. My body armor cracked. Emotions started leaking out of me onto the sidewalk like spaghetti water dripping into the sink from the bottom of a colander. In a flash I understood how she saw it— how her perception of being unintentionally "ignored" by me must *feel* for her. Her feelings were valid and right *for her.* But it wasn't the complete picture *of ME.*

"You want to know why?" I asked her. Without waiting for a response, I met her eyes. "I'll tell you why.

I'm an animal communicator. I talk to animals. It's who I am."

Her mouth now opened in disbelief. For a brief moment I really think this lady thought I was bat shit cray cray. Much to her credit, she stayed there—albeit a little squirmy—and listened.

"Do you want to know why I prefer to talk to animals over people? I'll tell you why." I blurted out—*without* waiting for a response. Tears started to fill my eyes. The holes in the proverbial colander seemed to swell as more emotional pain and heartache invisibly splashed onto the sidewalk between two strangers.

"It's because people suck.

"I have been hurt and felt shit on by far more people than animals. I have experienced and survived multiple types of abuse by people who were supposed to love and protect me. *AND* I have been mistreated, mishandled, and misunderstood by far more people than I care to admit. The truth is I feel safer next to a rattlesnake or a cheetah than I do most people."

The woman looked around. I don't know if she was looking for help, guidance, or a way out but she rose to the occasion. "Don't you be crying now," she clamored. "You gotta be strong now, you hear?!"

"I'm tired of being strong. It's exhausting. I want to trust. I want to love and feel safe but people suck and so many have let me down—" Tears were now trickling down my face, the sound of my words weakening and losing steam.

The woman's own armor joined mine on the sidewalk as she instinctively leaned in to give me a hug, then stopped short. Not wanting to assume anything, she decided to ask permission first. "Is it OK if I give you a hug?"

I nodded. The dog smiled. And we embraced.

In that brief encounter two strangers surrendered and took a chance. We took a chance for peace and understanding and created a heart connection despite commencing with hurt. A fitting tribute on any day but made even more beautiful on Memorial Day weekend.

The razor-sharp quills of our porcupine-like selves softened like overcooked spaghetti noodles as we politely introduced ourselves to one another. We talked about the state of *our* world. Not *her* world or *my* world, but *our world.* We owned *our* piece in perpetuating confusion and chaos through experiencing life from our hurts instead of our hearts. We talked about doggy diarrhea and how best to address it. We smiled at each other and relaxed.

With a newfound understanding of the other, we connected our hearts. It was easier now to hug again—more fluid, without hesitation or fear; without the noise of the world or the interference of our bruised egos. We changed. I'd like to think that the world will be a better place because of that moment and the ripple effect both of us will bring forward in our lives.

During that passing moment on the sidewalk, I realized that I'm *not* the only one who has suffered unimaginable hurt. The idea also finally registered that I may have also *caused* hurt to others— intended or not—hurt that I may never ever know.

I want to live in a more loving world surrounded by people willing to surrender to the same concept. If two shouting strangers can end up surrendering to love and understanding, I am hopeful that through God's grace and a dog's diarrhea, I'd like to believe there's hope for everyone to join the race!

The race to love.

Chapter 36

From Sibling Abuse to Sacred Self

Like a heart-wrenching moment frozen in history, I can remember exactly where I was, who I was with, and how I felt the first time I heard the words "sibling abuse." I have spent a little over six years unraveling what that meant and how deeply it affected me and my development. It has not been pretty or easy. Admittedly, there were days when I felt so alone and emotionally charged that I wished I could go back and put all the worms back in the can and seal the lid forever. Today I am so glad I couldn't.

I have learned that sibling abuse is a form of domestic violence that is a pervasive yet hidden issue that often goes unreported. The main reason is fear—fear of being blamed, punished, not believed, being afraid of the offending sibling, fear of upsetting or disappointing the parents or others and, as crazy as it sounds, the fear of getting the offender in trouble or disrupting the (dysfunctional) family dynamic! My sibling planted all those fears in me before I was old enough to speak.

I *was* a victim.
I *was* stifled.
I *was* afraid.
I *had* no resources.
I *didn't* know better.
I *was* filled with shame.
I *tried* to make sense of it.
I *tried* to reason it away.

~~~

I *had* to know more.

~~~

There *were* few resources.
There *was* disbelief.
There *was* disappointment.
There *was* so much pain.
There *was* isolation.
There *was* severe depression.
There *were* challenges.
There *was* disassociating.
There *was* dread.

It was like my life was built on quicksand, and I was just learning how to walk and talk all over again. I saw glimpses of a different life, a better life. I found others—others willing to admit trauma, abuse, neglect, and maltreatment at the hands of another family member. I heard things such as "It was in the past. I'm over it. I dealt with it." But the erratic behaviors and response to triggers said otherwise.

I kept at it. I kept unraveling. Reading. Writing. Talking. Walking. Discovering. Learning.

Again, I found others—others who talked openly about their experience and how it affected them. They were working a program of recovery. I listened. I heard my story being told by strangers—strangers who grew up similarly and had answers. The fellow travelers of ACA® welcomed me with open arms and called me "family." It was the first time in many, many years, when I heard that particular f word that I didn't cringe like a dog about to be hit with the newspaper.

"This" feels good.
Slowly,
I *became* a victor.
I *found* my voice.
I *spoke* my truth.
I *shed* my fears.
I *have* new resources.
I *know* better.
I *found* my dignity.

~~~

I re-awakened my sacred self.

Resources

Recommended Reading

Attached—The New Science of Adult Attachment and How It Can Help You Find and Keep Love by Amir Levine and Rachel Heller

What Happened to You—Conversations on Trauma, Resilience and Healing by Oprah Winfrey and Bruce D. Perry, M.D., Ph.D. (I recommend the audio version)

The Boy Who Was Raised as a Dog and Other Stories From a Child Psychiatrist's Notebook: What Traumatized Children Can Teach Us About Loss, Love and Healing by Bruce D. Perry, M.D., Ph.D., with Maia Szalavitz

Adult Children of Alcoholics®/Dysfunctional Families ACA® Fellowship Text (The Big Red Book) by ACA® WSO

Getting the Love You Want: A Guide for Couples by Harville Hendrix, Ph.D., and Helen LaKelly Hunt, Ph.D.

It Didn't Start With You: How Inherited Family Trauma Shapes Who We Are and How to End the Cycle by Mark Wolynn

Good Boundaries and Goodbyes: Loving Others Without Losing the Best of Who You Are by Lysa Terkeurst

Strengthening My Recovery: Meditations for Adult Children of Alcoholics/Dysfunctional Families by ACA® WSO

Between Two Kingdoms by Suleika Jaouad

Invisible Acts of Power: Channeling Grace in Your Everyday Life by Caroline Myss

The Touch of Healing: Energizing Body, Mind, and Spirit With the Art of Jin Shin Jyutsu by Alice Burmeister with Tom Monte

The Shadow in Our Lives: One Family's Recovery From Child Sexual Abuse by Tracey Wilson Heisler

The Dance of Anger: A Woman's Guide to Changing the Patterns of Intimate Relationships by Harriet Lerner, Ph.D.

Adult Children of Emotionally Immature Parents: How to Heal From Distant, Rejecting, or Self-Involved Parents by Linday C. Gibson, PsyD

The Myth of Normal: Trauma, Illness and Healing in a Toxic Culture by Gabor Maté, MD, with Daniel Maté

The Mindbody Prescription: Healing the Body, Healing the Pain by John E. Sarno, MD

The Divided Mind: The Epidemic of Mindbody Disorders by John E. Sarno, MD

The Secret Lives of Teeth: Understanding Emotional Influences on Oral Health by Meliors Simms

Audio
Songs for the Inner Child by Shaina Noll

YouTube
Gabor Maté: The Childhood Lie That's Ruining All of Our Lives

Gabor Maté: Abandonment Trauma

Vimeo
John Sarno Documentary

Self-Care and Supportive Healing Practices
Reiki

Integrated Energy Therapy® – www.learniet.com

Bowen Therapy also known as Bowenwork or Bowtech

Massage

Jin Shin Jyutsu

Yoga

Meditation

Sound Therapy

Color Therapy

Horse Therapy – Joan Summers

https://stepintojoyhealingarts.com/

Family Constellation Therapy – Douglas Economy,

https://douglaseconomy.com

Pranic Healing

Spending time outside in nature

Epsom salt baths with lavender, rosemary, or rose petals

6 Healing Sounds by Mantak Chia – YouTube

Acknowledgments

With my heart overflowing with gratitude, I must first acknowledge and thank my writers' group—Karen, Wendy, and Jan. They began as strangers, sometimes stood in as therapists, and created a safe space for me to unravel, tell my stories, and grow as a writer and a person. With their loving support, guidance, and encouragement, we have created an amazing book on a sensitive subject that is long overdue.

It would be near impossible to list *everyone* who helped unravel the stories, shape me, *and* the book, but here goes. My soul family has grown exponentially since undertaking this project. Much love and good health to Marie, Lori, Lisa, and Donna—you are the closest relationship to sisters I've experienced to date, and I am blessed to have you in my life. Abundant blessings to my soul brothers, Phil, Nelson, and Greg, who have shown me appropriate male love, compassion, and friendship—I love you guys! Thank you to my emotional support person and 'sperience buddy—I appreciate being part of your family more than you know. To the clients who have brought me into their lives like a welcome family member, I thank you for helping to fill my heart with love and hope on the darkest days. To the friends and strangers that held space during my constellation processes with Douglas, thank you! To Joan and the horses, I applaud and appreciate your healing work! I also thank all the fellow travelers in the various ACA® meetings I've attended this past year. Your authentic shares have given me hope for an emotionally healthier future and have assured me I am neither nuts nor alone.

Thank you, Fran, Gary, Maria, Barbara, and the rest of the IET® angels for keeping my energy clear during the sometimes arduous and painful process. Knowing you were holding space for me when I couldn't hold it for myself was exactly what I needed. May you receive the same tenfold.

A very special thank you to my animal Jin Shin Jyutsu teachers, buddies, classmates, and critters: Kelly, Adele, Terri, Linda, Susan, Norm, Dorothy, Allison, Robert, Toy (RIP), Shlomo, Benjamin, Jasper (RIP), Dawn the donkey, and so many others here and in spirit.

Thank you, Open Door Publications and Eric Labacz Design & Illustration, for all you've done to put this book together. It is an honor and a pleasure to walk this process with you. I am sending abundant blessings to you both.

Lastly, I thank the countless others who smiled, held a door, paid a compliment, made small talk, let me go ahead of them, bought me a coffee, or offered up another type of goodwill. Thank you for sharing love and helping to create the kind of world I really want to live in.

Kindness does matter.

About the Author

Sherri's childhood experience taught her that it's hard to hit a moving target. As such, she likes to stay active hiking, biking, playing softball, gardening, kayaking, camping, and whatever else calls to her sense of adventure in the moment. She's likely to be found playing outside, anywhere there may be animals, or well-behaved children—in any kind of weather. With more lives than a cat, and similar to the Phoenix, Sherri has transformed herself many times during this lifetime. Through it all one thing remains constant: her love for animals, nature, and spirit. Sherri currently makes her home in New Jersey with three dog-like cats—Chase, Spooky, and Boodah—calling all the shots.

Sherri's work experience is as diverse as a mutt's DNA. She is a retired Information Technology professional and former elected official who now spends her "spare time" working with animals and their people. She seamlessly blends traditional training as an Animal Control Officer, Reiki Master, and Integrated Energy Therapy® Master Instructor with her spiritual gift as a nondenominational minister and Animal Communicator to give animals a voice. Sherri also officiates weddings and funerals, guides rafting trips down the Lehigh River, is available for speaking engagements, leads her county's Animal Response Team and only God knows what else she'll add to the list before this book goes to print. People often ask her, "Is there anything you *can't* do?" Her answer is always the same. "I can't cut straight with scissors."

Sherri's first book, *All My Heroes Have, Fur, Fins & Feathers – An Animal Communicator's Healing Journey of Awakening,* is currently in seven countries, multiple libraries including the New Jersey Governor's Library at Drumthwacket, Amazon, and several retail outlets, including the trunk of her car.

In addition to continued travel to sacred spaces worldwide, Sherri plans to relocate to a less congested area off the grid that has "REAL WINTERS."